6|10

*ASHE Higher Education Report: Volume 35, Number 6*
*Kelly Ward, Lisa E. Wolf-Wendel, Series Editors*

# Access at the Crossroads: Learning Assistance in Higher Education

David R. Arendale

D1431979

**Access at the Crossroads: Learning Assistance in Higher Education**
David R. Arendale
ASHE Higher Education Report: Volume 35, Number 6
Kelly Ward, Lisa E. Wolf-Wendel, Series Editors

ISSN 1551-6970    electronic ISSN 1554-6306    ISBN 978-0-4706-4424-9

The **ASHE Higher Education Report** is part of the Jossey-Bass Higher and Adult Education Series and is published six times a year by Wiley Subscription Services, Inc., A Wiley Company, at Jossey-Bass, 989 Market Street, San Francisco, California 94103-1741.

**For subscription information,** see the Back Issue/Subscription Order Form in the back of this volume.

**CALL FOR PROPOSALS:** Prospective authors are strongly encouraged to contact Kelly Ward (kaward@wsu.edu) or Lisa Wolf-Wendel (lwolf@ku.edu). See "About the ASHE Higher Education Report Series" in the back of this volume.

Visit the Jossey-Bass Web site at **www.josseybass.com.**

Printed in the United States of America on acid-free recycled paper.

The **ASHE Higher Education Report** is indexed in CIJE: Current Index to Journals in Education (ERIC), Current Abstracts (EBSCO), Education Index/Abstracts (H.W. Wilson), ERIC Database (Education Resources Information Center), Higher Education Abstracts (Claremont Graduate University), IBR & IBZ: International Bibliographies of Periodical Literature (K.G. Saur), and Resources in Education (ERIC).

# Advisory Board

# Contents

# Executive Summary

Learning assistance often operates at the crossroads of the institution where academic affairs, student affairs, and enrollment management converge. Although learning assistance supports academic affairs with better-prepared students for academically rigorous courses, learning assistance also works in conjunction with student affairs to achieve higher affective and cognitive student development outcomes. At its best, learning assistance is carefully coordinated and supported with enrollment management programs that result in higher persistence rates and student success. This report describes the historic, diverse, and valuable activities in U.S. postsecondary education and opportunities that fall under the rubric of developmental education.

Although it has a presence in most postsecondary institutions, the expression of learning assistance is quite diverse. Campus needs and perceptions define the language of learning assistance, which explains a major reason for the wide variety of terms used to describe this field. The preferred term used in this report is "learning assistance," as it is commonly used and most inclusive of the various approaches and activities of the field.

## Major Issues and Questions in Learning Assistance

Postsecondary education confronts major trends in apparent conflict: increasing access to college to increase the number and diversity of people trained for employers, increasing academic standards of degree programs necessary for meeting requirements of a more highly skilled workforce, and accomplishing these objectives under heightened financial challenges resulting from diminished state and federal resources. The difference between increasing access and raising standards creates a gap. Learning assistance has bridged this gap in partnership with other campus services since the first colleges appeared. It has many names and forms. Learning assistance expresses itself quite differently between two-year and four-year institutions and even among those broad categories. This report identifies best practices that concurrently support higher education's goals of increased access and increased academic excellence.

This report explores difficult questions confronting learning assistance. What is the obligation of colleges and universities for providing assistance for students to attend college? Should students be regulated regarding where they should begin their academic career? Is learning assistance a civil rights issue for new students attending postsecondary education? Why did previous generations of students benefit from those services, even at the most prestigious public and private institutions in the United States? Are learning assistance needs better met by high schools and two-year institutions? What is the obligation of land-grant colleges to continue serving the needs of all students who are citizens of their states with whatever academic support services needed for their success? Do the postsecondary institution and society benefit from learning assistance?

A frequent approach by previous researchers focused on deficit needs of students labeled "at risk," "remedial," or "developmental" (Clowes, 1980; Rubin, 1987). These labels focus on students' perceived deficits. As a result, some campus policymakers are ambivalent or hold negative perceptions of the learning assistance field. This report presents a fresh approach that reinterprets current programs and opportunities for the future. Previous professional literature often stereotyped students accessing selected activities like developmental courses as seriously devoid of academic potential with phrases like "at-risk student" or "remedial or developmental student" (Roueche and Roueche, 1993; Tomlinson, 1989). Instead, this report uses the term "students who are academically underprepared in one or more academic content area" to describe the student population that enrolls in developmental courses. It more accurately states their academic capabilities. According to national research studies, most students who enroll in these courses do so in only a single academic content area

(National Center for Education Statistics, 2003). In other academic disciplines, they range from competent to expert learners. This report provides examples of students using learning assistance with a wide range of academic preparation levels, including those who are highly skilled and attend graduate or professional schools. For these students, learning assistance supplements, enriches, and inspires excellence. This report presents college students in a "talent development" model that builds on their strengths (Astin, 1984, 1985). Learning assistance expands the vision for serving a wider range of students and institutional purposes. Its best practices benefit all students.

## Actions to Improve Students' Success

This report identifies best practices in learning assistance that support both postsecondary access and academic excellence. These best practices yield improved student outcomes (Malnarich and others, 2003; Noel, Levitz, and Kaufmann, 1982; Roueche, Baker, and Roueche, 1984). These best practices encompass several areas in learning assistance: organization and administration, essential program components, critical instructional practices, important personnel practices, rigorous evaluation procedures, and necessary institutional practices, policies, and culture. Case studies of two-year and four-year institutions are interspersed throughout the report to provide examples of how these best practices have been implemented. The institutions were identified through previous research studies, competitive national awards programs, frequent citations in the professional literature, and identification by national leaders in the field (Boylan, 2002b; McCabe, 2003; McCabe and Day, 1998).

The report concludes with an examination of future opportunities for the field of learning assistance. Recommendations of this report invite action at all levels of postsecondary education:

Learning assistance professionals significantly increase their knowledge and skills to meet the needs of a more diverse student population, which includes obtaining advanced degrees specific to the work of learning assistance as well as joining professional associations that provide professional development—especially in program evaluation and new pedagogies for a more diverse student population.

Directors of learning assistance centers and departments adopt established best practices of the profession. Collaboration with other campus units expands services to the general student population as well as distance learners. Leveraging their vital knowledge and skills and participating on campuswide committees and task forces focusing on student learning outcomes, academic support, and student retention expands their influence and integrates learning assistance more clearly in the institution.

Senior campus administrators encourage learning assistance programs to be more active partners with campuswide student academic achievement and retention efforts. The investment of institutional resources for learning assistance yields higher dividends in higher student learning outcomes and persistence toward graduation.

Increased monitoring and evaluation by state policymakers regarding learning assistance activities such as developmental courses essential for some historically underrepresented students.

Competing national learning assistance associations create a new professional association employing more inclusive language, an expanded mission, and a broadened vision to serve postsecondary education.

Federal policymakers create a national center for research and dissemination of effective practices in postsecondary student success. A center focusing exclusively on college students, especially those who are historically underrepresented in postsecondary education, would complement recent efforts in K–12 education. In addition to collecting data and publishing reports, this new center would identify, validate, and disseminate evidence-based best practices.

These action steps, along with others listed in this report, can reposition learning assistance as a more essential and understood component to support student success.

Learning assistance is most effective operating at the confluence of the major institutional units of academic affairs, student affairs, and enrollment management. This high-profile, busy intersection of interests increases accountability of learning assistance to the campus community. All benefit from increased institutional and student outcomes. When properly funded, resourced, staffed, coordinated, and positioned, learning assistance provides access and excellence at the crossroads of the institution.

# Foreword

David Arendale's monograph, *Access at the Crossroads: Learning Assistance in Higher Education*, provides careful and thorough treatment of the many uses and manifestations of learning assistance in higher education. Learning assistance is a concept that is broad and sometimes ambiguous. It is easy to overlook and often misunderstood. This monograph clarifies the current issues facing the field of learning assistance. Arendale presents a very detailed and interesting history of learning assistance and how it has evolved in the larger context of higher education. The monograph also thoroughly treats the current and salient issues facing the field as well as provides a comprehensive review of best practices and models to consider in program development. The monograph stands at its own crossroads between theory and practice. The author presents the theoretical grounding from the literature that has shaped the field as well as presents how different theoretical perspectives inform practice.

What is learning assistance? What does it encompass? What role does it play in higher education? Before reading this monograph, I was not very aware of the broad scope of learning assistance and the extensive gamut of programs it encompasses. *Learning assistance* is a term that has often been associated with students' deficit understanding—that is, students coming into higher education with shortcomings in their educational backgrounds and then needing learning assistance to navigate the rigors of higher education and to remediate deficiencies. Learning assistance activities range from skill development and tutoring to remedial courses and technology assistance.

Learning assistance moves far beyond simply a deficit orientation toward learning and development, and Arendale explains and delineates a more comprehensive view.

The book provides an extensive historical overview of learning assistance. Examining this history allows the reader to see how the negative associations with learning assistance have evolved. Sometimes referred to as "developmental" and "remedial" education, the role, purpose, and place of learning assistance in higher education are often controversial, given the mixed perspectives on whether learning assistance is something colleges and universities should even provide. The historical perspective Arendale provides equips the reader with knowledge about how learning assistance has developed in different time periods in higher education. Arendale's historical overview offers readers information about the origins of learning assistance and its longstanding presence in higher education, dating back to colonial colleges. As long as higher education has existed, students' preparation and aptitude have differed. Learning assistance has always had a role and place in higher education and likely always will. It is particularly important to understand the historical origins of the contemporary landscape of higher education and the role of learning assistance, given the desire to accommodate diverse students.

Many questions exist about learning assistance in higher education. What role does learning assistance play in higher education? Do people who need learning assistance merit college standing? If students are ill prepared, should they be in college? How is learning assistance manifest in different types of institutions? In response to these and other questions, some campuses have eliminated or outsourced learning assistance programs, while others have expanded the role and scope of learning assistance. Regardless of how campuses respond, learning assistance, given its broad scope and purpose, continues to be a contemporary issue that can be vexing to faculty and administrators. Arendale provides the resources faculty and administrators need to take action on their campuses on issues related to learning assistance. The author is careful to provide examples from a broad range of institutions in terms of type, size, and mission. The book also does an excellent job of making the case for a broad-based perspective of learning assistance that is grounded in learning and development as a way to meet the needs of an ever-diverse student body.

The title of the monograph, *Access at the Crossroads*, suggests that learning assistance sits at the juncture of important issues facing higher education—diversity and access, student' access and success, student affairs and academic affairs. Arendale details these crossroads throughout the monograph and provides readers with resources and a response to navigate the crossroads. The monograph adopts a student development and learning approach that focuses on an open perspective instead of a deficit approach.

The contemporary landscape of higher education is one marked by diversity and fiscal constraints, leaving learning assistance programs extremely vulnerable and increasingly necessary at the same time. Arendale's use of campus-based examples from a variety of institutional types of how learning assistance programs are organized and developed provides readers with helpful resources to guide and develop learning assistance programs. Practitioners looking to potentially add, expand, or amend campus-based learning assistance will find the monograph informative. Practitioners will also find helpful the delineation of the historical and contemporary issues facing the field to convey the importance of programmatic issues. Researchers will find the monograph helpful in its broad scope and connection to other related issues in higher education, including diversity, civil rights, and students' success. When read in conjunction with other ASHE monographs, Arendale's book is particularly helpful in illustrating the connections between students' success, diversity, and learning assistance. Readers might find it useful to look at this monograph in conjunction with other recent ASHE monographs that address related issues—for example, Marybeth Walpole's *Economically and Educationally Challenged Students in Higher Education: Access to Outcomes* (2007) and Laura Perna and Scott Thomas's *Theoretical Perspectives on Student Success: Understanding the Contribution of the Disciplines* (2008). These monographs in conjunction with Arendale's new one address some of the nuances that call for understanding of theory and practice related to the multiple manifestations of learning assistance in higher education today. David Arendale's treatment of learning assistance, contemporary issues, and future prospects in *Access at the Crossroads: Learning Assistance in Higher Education* is sure to be useful to researchers, practitioners, and students of higher education.

**Lisa E. Wolf-Wendel**
Series Editor

# Acknowledgments

I learned long ago that no one achieves anything significant in life without the active support and encouragement of others. Many people helped me with this publication. I thank my editor, Kelly Ward, for her patience, guidance, and encouragement. Her comments as well as those of the external reviewers were essential.

My colleagues in the Department of Postsecondary Teaching and Learning at the University of Minnesota have taught me the multiple identities we possess and our boundless capabilities to learn and achieve. I am indebted to Jeanne Higbee for her mentorship. She gives so much to her students, colleagues, and the profession.

Many colleagues and friends outside the university were significant partners and supporters. Hunter Boylan and colleagues at the National Center for Developmental Education in Boone, North Carolina, provided important encouragement and access to resource materials. I have learned much from other leaders in the field, including Frank Christ and Martha Maxwell. Colleagues in my professional associations were important sources of knowledge and inspiration, and I learned much from my peers and mentors in the National Association for Developmental Education, the College Reading and Learning Association, and the National College and Learning Center Association.

I express my appreciation to learning assistance colleagues at other institutions and undergraduate students in my history courses. My colleagues teach me great lessons about the field. My students coach me about how to be a better teacher and facilitator of the learning process. They are gracious as I experiment with new forms of learning assistance in the classroom and provide feedback of what works for them.

This monograph is lovingly dedicated to John and Leota Arendale, my parents, who taught me to love reading, honor God, pursue education, and serve others. It is also dedicated to Martha Maxwell, who set the standard and vision for learning assistance. She had a long life of rich experiences and shared her wisdom with so many of us.

Published online in Wiley InterScience
(www.interscience.wiley.com) • DOI: 10.1002/aehe.3506

# Introduction

LEARNING ASSISTANCE MEETS THE DEMANDS of rigorous college courses through highly varied activities and approaches. The historic role of learning assistance in the larger scope of U.S. higher education is significant though sometimes low profile. Learning assistance bridges access for a more diverse student body. From students' perspectives, it helps them meet institutional academic expectations and achieve personal learning goals. From the institution's perspective, it expands access to the institution and supports higher expectations for academic excellence.

There is no universal manifestation of learning assistance. On some campuses, it expresses itself through noncredit activities such as tutorial programs, peer study groups, study strategy workshops, computer-based learning modules, or drop-in learning centers. Other institutions add to these activities by offering remedial and developmental courses, study strategy courses, and other services. A few colleges support learning assistance for graduate and professional school students through workshops on dissertation writing and effective studying, strategies for graduate school examinations, and preparation for licensure exams at the conclusion of their professional school programs. Students from broad demographic backgrounds access one or more of these services from all levels of academic preparation and at various times during their academic career. The diverse language used to describe learning assistance depends on institutional culture and history. Some terms associated with these activities throughout history include *preparatory, remedial, compensatory, developmental,* and *enrichment,* to name just a few. *Learning assistance* provides a universal description for this wide variety of expressions, activities, and approaches. It is the term used most generally in this report.

A myth persists that learning assistance serves only "developmental students." Actually, no such thing as a "developmental student" exists. Rather, it is more accurate to say that some students are not academically prepared for college-level work in one or more academic content areas (English, mathematics, or writing) or in specific skills such as reading or study strategies. The relative need and usefulness of learning assistance for an individual student depends on the overall academic rigor of the institution, the subject matter studied, or even how one faculty member teaches a particular course compared with another from the same academic department. Therefore, the same individual could be a major consumer of learning assistance at one institution and not at another or even in one academic department and not another in the same institution. The need for learning assistance services is not a characteristic or universal defining attribute of the student; it depends on the conditions and expectations of the specific learning environment for a particular course. All college students are on a continuum between novice and master learner. Learning assistance serves students located along this continuum through a wide range of activities and services. The same student is often located at different places on multiple continuum lines simultaneously, one for each academic context and skill area.

Certain groups of students bring less social capital with them to college—students from low socioeconomic backgrounds, first-generation college students, and historically underrepresented students of color. Learning assistance services, especially developmental courses, are essential for overcoming disadvantaged backgrounds. Learning assistance is essential for providing access to a broad range of institutions.

The student groups that had not traditionally attended college before have a variety of overlapping identities, some of which pose barriers that impede success in college. Walpole (2007) analyzed this population and names one group "economically and educationally challenged." "All [economically and educationally challenged] students, regardless of gender, race, or ethnicity, face challenges in accessing, persisting, and graduating from college. The intersections of these identity statuses and educational processes and outcomes are non-linear and deserve additional attention" (p. x). Walpole states that challenges for these students are not the result of a failure to try or that they are somehow inferior to the students from dominate cultures. "Rather these students must cope with a structure and a system that defines merit in ways that do not privilege them" (p. 15).

Learning assistance can help these new students overcome the barriers that might limit their chances for succeeding in postsecondary education. Deciding whether to curtail or eliminate credit-based learning assistance such as developmental courses does not just affect campus economics or perceptions of institutional prestige. It is not a race- and class-neutral decision. This report illustrates how a wide range of students at most institutions, regardless of their classification, use noncredit learning assistance activities such as tutoring, study groups, learning assistance centers, and the like. Lack of access to credit-based learning assistance, however, raises issues of class, race, and culture. It is a serious decision to tell essentially an entire group of students who share common demographic identities such as first-generation college students, students of color, and low socioeconomic students to begin their college career at a two-year college, while privileged students can begin wherever they want. No one quite says it that way. The impact is the same, however, if the needed resources are not available and the campus culture is not welcoming to the new students. The risk is de facto resegregation of postsecondary education in the United States and all the disastrous results for individuals and society that would occur (Bowen, Chingos, and McPherson, 2009).

Most aspects of learning assistance vary greatly across institutions. Depending on the institution, the leader of the learning assistance program could be a tenured faculty member or affiliated staff person, which affects perceptions, funding, and the integration of learning assistance programs at the institution. Some learning assistance programs are centralized in the institution, while others are decentralized and assigned to an individual department or unit in academic affairs, student affairs, or enrollment management. Still others report to multiple units. Operating at the crossroads of academic affairs, student affairs, and enrollment management is the most effective and strategic location for learning assistance to benefit the institution and its students—thus the inspiration for the name of this monograph: *Access at the Crossroads: Learning Assistance in Higher Education.*

Its location at the confluence of academic affairs, student affairs, and enrollment management often places learning assistance in the center of great controversy and puts it under tremendous scrutiny. The current economic crisis amplifies the debate of the role of learning assistance. Who belongs in college? Where should they start their academic experience? What resources are needed for their success? This is the subject of the second chapter.

The following chapter presents a comprehensive history of learning assistance. Some perceive learning assistance as a relatively recent phenomenon created for the new student populations attending college after World War II. Since its inception, however, learning assistance has had a presence in U.S. colleges and universities. Although the profile of students and the menu of services have changed over time, learning assistance has a long and pervasive history with U.S. postsecondary education.

"Current Nature and Scope of Learning Assistance" explores how its expressions lead indirectly to its mystery and misunderstanding. Although this report uses the term "learning assistance" to describe the field, institutions across the United States employ more than 150 titles for the centers and departments that provide these services. An advantage of learning assistance is the strength of contextualizing itself for each institution to meet its needs. Sometimes the activities serve students before they enroll in college-level courses through high school–college bridge programs or coordinating curricula between secondary and postsecondary teachers. Other colleges instead focus learning assistance activities after students arrive through remedial and developmental college credit courses. Other colleges provide only noncredit activities such as tutoring, small study groups, and drop-in learning centers. Many colleges do all of these activities. The chapter frames and organizes these approaches and evaluates the likelihood of success in achieving desired institutional and student outcomes.

The following chapter builds on this foundational information by exploring best practices of learning assistance and challenges for implementing them. These practices and illustrating case studies were identified through national studies by leaders in the field (Boylan, 2002b; McCabe, 2000, 2003; McCabe and Day, 1998; Roueche and Roueche, 1999). The final chapter focuses on the future of learning assistance and action steps for all stakeholders—learning assistance professionals, directors of learning assistance programs, upper-level campus administrators, professional associations that represent the profession, and state and national policymakers. Complex challenges require comprehensive actions and coordinated solutions from these stakeholders.

The next chapter, "Current Challenges and Controversies for Learning Assistance," frames the contemporary field by examining the issues and challenges that confront it. Differences of opinion exist in postsecondary education about the history, value, and importance of learning assistance. And the intense financial crisis nearly all institutions face fuels the critical examination of the role of learning assistance.

# Current Challenges and Controversies for Learning Assistance

A VARIETY OF CONTEMPORARY CHALLENGES affect the field of learning assistance. The first is inadequate knowledge of the long history and pervasive nature of learning assistance. Lack of knowledge of its role in history places the field in a precarious position, creating a context for challenges related to perceptions and values concerning learning assistance. The language used to describe the field is itself an issue and too often a catalyst for opposition. The issue of stigma affects students most often when they enroll in developmental courses. The role of learning assistance with supporting access and equity in postsecondary education is controversial when it is argued that some students should be directed to enter college only through two-year institutions because of their need to enroll in developmental courses. This issue becomes more complicated when a significant number of those course takers are poor and students of color. To what extent does higher education resegregate itself along economic and ethnic lines? What is the consequence for them and for the greater society? And why does any college student need additional academic preparation, as he or she should already be prepared for college based on graduation from a high school? Why spend scarce institutional resources and pay for something twice? Examining these issues is the objective for this chapter.

## Lack of Knowledge About the History of Learning Assistance

Although learning assistance is a significant and sometimes controversial element in higher education, it is underreported by many historians of postsecondary education. A review of the professional literature demonstrates that some higher education historians ignore and others lightly record historical events concerning learning assistance in U.S. postsecondary education. Although the learning assistance community has published numerous articles, dissertations, and monographs (Lundell and Higbee, 2002), those writing broad histories of higher education in the United States have paid little attention to this area and the students involved (Arendale, 2001, 2002a, 2002b; Brubacher and Rudy, 1976; Lucas, 2006; Jeynas, 2007; Rudy, 1996; Stahl and King, 2009).

As discussed later in this report, a review of this component of higher education documented that many students throughout U.S. history were involved with learning assistance activities such as academic tutoring, enrollment in remedial or developmental courses, and participation in learning assistance center services. At times, learning assistance programs involved more than half of all college students at an institution (Canfield, 1889; Ignash, 1997; Maxwell, 1997; Shedd, 1932). The lines become blurred as students simultaneously enroll in courses at the developmental and college level in different academic subjects. Academic preparedness is not a characteristic of the student; rather, it is a condition relative to a particular academic course during the same academic term. It is inaccurate to designate students as "remedial" or "developmental," for they may be competent or expert in one academic content area and needing learning assistance credit and noncredit services in another.

Kammen (1997) provides an explanation for underreporting the history of learning assistance, identifying "historical amnesia" as a potential cause. Quoting Ralph Ellison, he says, "Perhaps this is why we possess two basic versions of American history: one [that] is written and as neatly stylized as ancient myth, the other unwritten and as chaotic and full of contradictions, changes of pace, and surprises as life itself" (p. 164). Distortions of memory occur for a variety of reasons, not only for cynical or manipulative motives (Kammen, 1997). The researcher engages in a long discussion concerning the similarities and differences between the "heritage syndrome" and true history: "The heritage syndrome, if I may call it that, almost seems to be a predictable but certainly nonconspiratorial response—an impulse to remember what is attractive or flattering and to ignore all the rest. Heritage is comprised of those aspects of history that we cherish and affirm. As an alternative to history, heritage accentuates the positive but sifts away what is problematic. One consequence is that the very pervasiveness of heritage as a phenomenon produces a beguiling sense of serenity about the well being of history" (p. 220).

Acknowledging the role and importance of learning assistance presents uncomfortable statements about higher education:

Academic bridge programs are necessary for students to adjust to a college environment for which few are prepared.

Student subpopulations other than the most privileged often need academic support systems to increase their chances for success resulting from disadvantaged and deprived backgrounds.

The need for learning assistance indicts the efficacy and effectiveness of elementary and secondary education.

Scarce financial resources and personnel are necessary to meet the needs of students who are academically underprepared.

Some students who drop out of college could have been retained through an effective learning assistance program.

Lack of knowledge about the history of learning assistance also contributes to current challenges for the field. For example, it is easier to curtail or eliminate learning assistance activities if its historic importance for support and access to postsecondary education is not understood. As explored in the next chapter, learning assistance was an essential asset for colleges to support student achievement and persistence. During the current period of financial emergency confronting many institutions, nonessential services are subject to reduction or elimination. This topic of historical amnesia related to learning assistance is more fully explored in other publications (see, for example, Arendale, 2001, 2002a).

## Challenges of Shifting Perceptions and Values

So far this chapter has explored historical amnesia about learning assistance. This section turns to shifting perceptions and values dramatically affecting the field and the students it serves. The diversity of language describing the field contributes to misunderstanding (Arendale, 2005b). As others outside the profession define it based on its murky language, some stigmatize learning assistance participants and those providing the service. This characterization is ironic, for contemporary learning assistance serves the most privileged students as well as those who have the most disadvantages. Perception of stigma leads some to argue that the presence of students who are academically underprepared for some academic areas undermine the entire education enterprise. The natural extension of this perception leads critics to argue that some students do not belong in college and that therefore learning assistance is unnecessary. The first challenge considered is this section is the language describing the field. This misunderstanding is at the root of most subsequent challenges.

## Perceptions of Learning Assistance Framed by the Language Describing It

This field has used a variety of terms to describe itself over the past two hundred years: academic preparatory programs, remedial education, compensatory education, learning assistance, developmental education, and access programs, just to name the major terms. In most areas of higher education, the progression of names is a historical process, with one term dominating the literature. In this field, these terms are frequently used simultaneously and interchangeably (Arendale, 2005b). Language reflects culture and confusion existing in the culture (Rice, 1980). In this report, the term "learning assistance" describes the broad and highly diverse field.

Terms that were generally accepted in the past or present such as "compensatory," "remedial," or "developmental" become stigmatized later (Arendale, 2005b; Jehangir, 2002; Pedelty, 2001). Some words assume new and different meanings based on the personal agenda of a few (Clowes, 1980; Rubin, 1987). Words are politicized by accepting a different meaning or value because a small group in society affixes negative status to the word. A powerful display of this phenomenon is local or state policymakers who promote a negative stereotype of remedial education and compensatory education (Clowes, 1980; Higbee, 1996; Payne and Lyman, 1996; Soliday, 2002). Negative perceptions grow with use of the term "developmental education."

A careful review of the history of learning assistance reveals that terms used to describe it fifty years ago are now increasingly viewed negatively.

It is not surprising that some policymakers are confused about a profession seemingly unable to name itself consistently and clearly advocate for the field. Learning assistance professionals must be clear and proactive about defining the field, or it will be subject to definition and labeling by ill-informed outsiders often using antiquated and inaccurate words to define the practice (Rubin, 1987). In recent years, collaborative work among several professional associations produced several glossaries of key terms related to learning assistance (Rubin, 1991; Arendale and others, 2007; Arendale, 2009).

Language used initially for students served by learning assistance changed and was later interpreted to label them negatively (Ignash, 1997). Nor were the leaders of learning assistance programs immune to the negative label. Some perceived students in terms of their deficits (Tomlinson, 1989). The result of such language choices led some education leaders to no longer support learning assistance services, especially developmental courses (Jehangir, 2002). Especially at four-year institutions, campus leaders were hard-pressed to enroll large numbers of "remedial students" or "developmental students."

This report follows an admonition from the American Psychological Association in the sixth edition of its publication style manual (2010) to avoid labeling people and to put the person first when describing a characteristic about him or her. Therefore, the term "developmental student," is inaccurate and is not used. Rather, the phrase "students academically underprepared in one or more academic content areas" is a better descriptor for those enrolled in developmental courses. This phrase does not judge their academic readiness for other college-level courses. Use of terms like "developmental student," "remedial student," "compensatory student," and the like imply lack of capacity or competency. A wide range of students from varying levels of academic preparation use noncredit learning assistance services. In addition to supplementing courses, learning assistance can also enrich undergraduate and graduate learning. Labeling students accessing such noncredit services is impossible, as any member of the student body can—and often does—use them.

The term "learning assistance" is used in this report because of its inclusiveness and accurate depiction of the purpose and activities employed. It is not limited to particular student population groups based on their level of academic preparation. Another term used to describe this field (particularly in the United Kingdom) is "access education" (Burke, 2002; Fulton and others, 1981).Through this frame, access programs incorporate traditional learning assistance activities such as tutoring, developmental courses, and others that prepare students for success in rigorous college-level courses. Learning assistance centers support success in rigorous classes as well as supplemental learning venues for any learner to deepen knowledge of academic content through computer-based learning modules, study groups to deepen knowledge and skill in a course, and other activities. Access activities not typically included in the current learning assistance paradigm are first-year experience programs, new student orientation, services for students with disabilities, TRIO programs, instructional professional development for the teaching staff, and other services promoting student success. A challenge with the term "access education," however, is the inaccurate perception that it focuses only on activities serving students entering the institution and not supporting and enriching their college experience through timely graduation. This report does not attempt to rename the profession though it does promote broader responsibilities, inclusive language, and new partners in higher education (see the last chapter of this report). The issue of negative perceptions of the language used to define the field leads to the next challenge, potential stigma for the field and the students it serves.

### Stigma for Enrolling in Developmental Courses
Scholars at several institutions conducted research studies concerning students' perceptions of learning assistance programs, especially developmental credit courses. Research indicated negative stigma was attached, regardless of voluntary or mandated enrollment (Higbee, Lundell, and Arendale, 2005; Pedelty, 2001; Valeri-Gold and others, 1997). Perceptions of stigma have plagued learning assistance throughout history. Some believe stigma increases restrictions and curtails programs, especially at public four-year institutions (Barefoot, 2003; Jehangir, 2002; Martinez, Snider, and Day, 2003).

Various factors contribute to stigma: (1) mandatory enrollment in developmental courses; (2) new students placed in cohorts identified for academic risk; (3) use of terms such as "at-risk students," "high-risk students," "developmental students," and "academically disadvantaged students," all of which represent a negative condition characterizing students' academic abilities and potential; (4) public policy fights over admission of students perceived to be academically underprepared; and (5) memories of emotional hazing in previous schools.

Students often experience two concurrent emotions regarding learning assistance. They appreciate the help of learning assistance personnel to strengthen their academic skills, are grateful the institution admits them, and appreciate varied learning assistance activities. On the other hand, contact with these activities inadvertently leads to self-stigmatization because they recognize that not all students use the same learning assistance activities, especially developmental courses. Students enrolled in developmental courses recognize their academic profile is lower than that of other students at the institution. Diminished self-esteem and believing they do not belong often emerge. Sometimes anger is directed at others and themselves, leading to self-sabotaging academic behavior. This chain of events results in premature academic failure and departure from the institution (Higbee, Lundell, and Arendale, 2005).

When stigma attaches itself to language describing learning assistance and the students served by it, institutional leaders can lose interest and curtail these programs, especially at four-year institutions (Jehangir, 2002). Insufficient services diminish students' academic success. The issue of language and stigma leads to the next controversy in this chapter. Are students' rights abridged by institutions' failing to provide them the same services provided to students in previous generations?

### Civil Rights, Equity Issues, and Learning Assistance

Do students have a right to sufficient academic support at every higher education institution? Are students' civil rights abridged when the services are not offered? This controversial issue probes the need for learning assistance, credit and noncredit, at all institutions because of issues of equity and equal access. Reframing learning assistance for this purpose expands the need for comprehensive services. Because education is considered a reserved right of the states, federal civil rights laws do not currently apply, but the question of whether this equity issue is covered by the equal opportunity clause of the U.S. Constitution is open to debate and potential litigation. In addition, the original federal charters for land-grant institutions specified service to all students residing in a state. Many such colleges and universities have instituted selective admission policies excluding automatic admission of any resident student, and it raises similar equity issues (Ancheta, 2007).

Learning assistance services such as developmental courses are essential for students experiencing extreme academic difficulty in one or more academic content areas. These students are often from low socioeconomic or other groups that have been historically underrepresented in postsecondary education. Walpole (2007) names them "economically and educationally challenged." This controversy changes the issue from whether these students benefit from learning assistance to a question of whether failure to provide access programs violates their civil rights because they need these services for success (Miksch, 2005, 2008). A legal term describing absence of services for one population while available to another is "disproportionate impact." Does failing to provide essential learning assistance services at the institution of choice for these students affect them more negatively than the larger student population that is better academically prepared because they come from privileged backgrounds?

When students attended U.S. colleges in the 1700s and 1800s, academic preparatory academies and remedial and developmental courses were offered at all institutions, even elite private colleges. These offerings were necessary as a result of nonexistent or poor-quality private or public education. When privileged students were able to access quality public or private education before college, many institutions curtailed or eliminated developmental courses. The "new students" often represent first-generation college students, students of color, and those underprepared academically because they attended poorly funded and underperforming urban or rural public school districts (Kozol, 1991).

Based on the largest national study on learning assistance, one-third of students enrolled in developmental courses are students of color, mostly African Americans and Hispanic Americans (Boylan, Bonham, and Bliss, 1994). At two-year institutions, 29 percent of students enrolled in these courses were African American and Hispanic American. The proportion grew to 37 percent at four-year institutions. The removal of these courses at four-year colleges and universities significantly affects students of color, as they are more likely to enroll than white students (Boylan, Bonham, and Bliss, 1994). African American students are more than twice as likely to enroll in these classes at two-year institutions, compared with their proportion of the student population. At four-year institutions, the rate soars to three times more likely to enroll in the courses (Boylan, Bonham, and Bliss, 1994).

If students from economically and educationally challenged backgrounds are admitted to an institution with selective admission policies, they are often denied the same services previously provided to an earlier generation of privileged students at the same institution. Why is it acceptable to treat these two student populations differently? Both had the same need because of inadequate secondary school education. Why was it necessary to provide developmental courses for the first group in the past but deny those same services to the second group from economically and educationally challenged backgrounds in this generation?

Failure of these students to complete higher education is a concern not only for them and their families. Society pays a heavy price economically and socially for their failure (Belfield and Levin, 2007; Bowen, Chingos, and McPherson, 2009). This failure is another reason that learning assistance is a public policy issue.

Miksch (2005) investigates unequal availability of college preparatory and Advanced Placement programs in U.S. high schools. The majority of well-funded suburban public schools offer these programs, while less than half of high schools in rural and urban areas do. These courses are essential for successfully passing AP examinations that colleges use for awarding free college credit and fulfill other first-year classes without expense or time. This advantage is denied to those not taking or passing AP examinations because of inaccessibility to college preparatory classes. A trained attorney and education policy expert, Miksch concludes, "this access to AP is a critical civil right issues" (2005, p. 227). The same principle applies to learning assistance. Curtailment or elimination of learning assistance activities, especially developmental courses, is not a neutral decision by four-year institutions. Providing these services, including developmental courses, to an earlier generation of privileged white students and then eliminating them for first-generation students from low socioeconomic backgrounds effectively closes the admissions door to them or neglects their needs if they are admitted (Boylan, Saxon, White, and Erwin, 1994). In either case, postsecondary education becomes more stratified and segregated. Cross (1976) argued these courses are essential for affirmative action and educational opportunity.

When access to essential learning assistance services is diminished, new access and equity questions arise. Who belongs in college? Where should they begin their academic career? Should some applicants be permitted to attend college, regardless of its location or level?

### *Who Really Belongs in College? Where Might They Begin?*

Contextualizing the historic role of learning assistance, those who work in learning assistance programs neither determine admission criteria nor set academic standards (Boylan, 1995a). Admissions officers, administrators, faculty committees, and state higher education executive offices are responsible for those decisions. Once standards are set, however, it is the job of learning assistance faculty and staff to ensure students meet or exceed them. The need for learning assistance was created as soon as the first college opened its doors to those prepared to pass the admissions examination and those who were not. These criteria de facto divided students into two groups: those admitted normally and those admitted provisionally. Provisional students need additional academic assistance and enrichment. As the upcoming history chapter documents, many students attending U.S. colleges in the 1700s and 1800s participated in learning assistance activities before admission as well as throughout their academic career (Boylan and White, 1987; Brier, 1984; Craig, 1997).

Nearly all institutions historically offered developmental courses. During the past twenty years, eight states have or are in process of eliminating developmental courses at public four-year colleges. At the same time, thirty states rejected similar legislation (Abraham and Creech, 2000). These mixed results indicate that some states are mandating the shift of the courses from public four-year institutions to community colleges (Hankin, 1996). Shifting the developmental courses often occurs at the level of the campus or state system. For example, in Missouri no state legislation required shifting these courses.

Three decades ago, the University of Missouri system eliminated the courses. State four-year and two-year institutions informally assumed them.

During the past quarter century, community colleges assumed primary responsibility for vocational programs, workplace literacy, displaced worker retraining, certificate programs, and others. Their primary role of preparing students for transfer to senior institutions expanded (Cohen and Brawer, 2002; Townsend and Dougherty, 2007). Traditional boundaries between community and technical colleges blurred as costly technical programs were offered at community colleges. These expanded curricular responsibilities required community colleges to invest in more buildings, equipment, and faculty members for expensive high-demand certificate and associate degree programs in response to local needs of citizens and employers. Increased prestige of community colleges and heightened stigma concerning developmental courses led a growing number of community college leaders to reject increased responsibility for them (McGrath and Spear, 1994; Oudenhoven, 2002). Community colleges are placed in a double bind to maintain their traditional open admission access and increase academic standards necessary for the new curricular offerings. Some leaders question how both can be maintained while dealing with a large influx of students needing developmental courses formerly offered at four-year colleges (Perin, 2006).

Some policymakers direct students with academic preparation requiring developmental courses to begin their college career at junior and community colleges. These students might be accepted for transfer to the senior institution if their junior college academic profile warrants. The transfer process from community colleges to senior institutions has numerous challenges. As a result, the students are placed at higher risk for academic failure than those who begin their careers in four-year schools (Pascarella and Terenzini, 1991, 2005; Tinto, 1993).

Considerable effort has been made with articulation agreements among two-year and four-year institutions. The transfer process is not transparent, however, and the rate of completing an undergraduate degree is lower for students who begin at a two-year institution than for those beginning at a four-year institution, even when controlling for other variables (Pascarella and Terenzini, 1991, 2005; Tinto, 1993). This finding was confirmed through a national study based on data from the National Library of Education (Boesel, 1999). Barriers to success for transfer students include not accepting or requiring them to repeat courses previously completed and the turbulence experienced by students as they move from one academic environment to another. It is common for students to experience academic difficulty and earn lower grade averages as a result at the senior institution (Eggleston and Laanan, 2001).

With institutional resources, including learning assistance, students from a wide range of ethnic and socioeconomic backgrounds can be accepted and supported for academic success. Learning assistance, especially developmental courses, have been significant resources for students of color (Boylan, Bonham, and Bliss, 1994). These services along with other institutional supports increase the likelihood of higher student achievement and persistence toward graduation (Boylan, Saxon, White, and Erwin, 1994).

# Financial Challenges for Learning Assistance

This cluster of challenges centers on financial pressures that confront learning assistance and the campuses that offer it. Ignorance and misunderstanding of learning assistance place it in a precarious position as campus administrators make difficult budget decisions. As a result of the perceptions of stigma and limited research on effective practices, the field has faced intense scrutiny throughout recent history. As a result, some learning assistance activities such as developmental courses are eliminated and their functions hoped to be assumed by four-year institutions with less selective admissions policies and two-year colleges. Some raise the issue of why tax dollars should be spent on academic preparation activities that should have been addressed in high school.

### *Impact of Institutional Mission Differentiation on Learning Assistance*

Economic challenges since the 1970s, especially among public institutions, have intensified. Land-grant institutions debate how to balance their historic egalitarian mission serving all state residents while curtailing programs and raising admission standards. Institutional leaders increasingly employ institutional "mission differentiation" to reign in costs and focus resources on the institution (Slaughter and Rhoades, 2004). Mission differentiation recognizes institutions with special programmatic offerings and targeted student populations. Selective college admission policies lead some to question the need for comprehensive learning assistance services, especially developmental courses.

Preliminary analysis of mission differentiation reveals unannounced and unanticipated outcomes for learning assistance (Bastedo and Gumport, 2003; Gumport and Bastedo, 2001; Slaughter and Rhoades, 2004). Analysis of learning assistance policy in Massachusetts and New York confirmed that mission differentiation led institutions to terminate academic programs, eliminate remedial or developmental courses, and promote honors colleges. The result is stratification of academic program opportunity in the state. Prestigious and high-demand academic programs were offered at fewer institutions than before. For students, stratification encouraged higher admissions standards at upper-tier institutions. As a result, students had fewer choices for postsecondary education (Bastedo and Gumport, 2003; Gumport and Bastedo, 2001; Slaughter and Rhoades, 2004).

Another result was curtailment of developmental courses at upper-tier institutions in the state system (Bastedo and Gumport, 2003; Gumport and Bastedo, 2001). Developmental courses are often a key ingredient in providing access and success for historically underrepresented students. Bastedo and Gumport (2003) concluded that more intense analysis is warranted before systemic changes occur to avoid or at least predict major changes in the stratification of students' opportunity to attend postsecondary education and the student support systems needed for their success.

As more historically underrepresented students from diverse racial and socioeconomic backgrounds seek admission, important learning assistance infrastructures are dismantled (Bastedo and Gumport, 2003). Mission differentiation assumes incorrectly that college aspirants are more academically prepared, and institutional leaders therefore conclude that developmental credit courses and other traditional learning assistance activities are not needed. Increasingly, public four-year institutions curtail or eliminate developmental courses with the expectation that students needing such instruction easily access them at a community college (Bastedo and Gumport, 2003; Gumport and Bastedo, 2001; Slaughter and Rhoades, 2004). This option requires a local community college. Most students do not have the financial resources or time to commute long distances for such classes. These students often are financially disadvantaged and possess little free time. They cannot commute to multiple institutions for courses while maintaining a job (or two) to pay for college and support a family. Based on a national dataset, students who attend multiple institutions are less likely to graduate from college than those who begin at the intended degree-awarding institution (Adelman, 2006).

Mission differentiation raises a new set of questions and conflicts in postsecondary education (McPherson and Schapiro, 1999). Access to higher education shifts to access to what form of education and under what conditions. Differentiation among institutions increases stratification in society (Anderson, Daugherty, and Corrigan, 2005).

### *Public Tax Dollars and Learning Assistance*

Advocates for eliminating learning assistance claim that students should have developed their skills and knowledge in high school and that therefore no need exists for developmental courses or other services at colleges, especially at four-year institutions. Why should taxpayers pay for something twice? Actually, taxpayers have not paid for such services even once. Depending on the national data used, between one-third and one-half of secondary students complete a college-bound program of study while in high school (Manzo, 2007; Perkins, Kleiner, Roey, and Brown, 2004). About three-quarters of high school graduates enroll in college (Adelman, 2004). The gap between those who attend college and the smaller percent that complete preparation for college demonstrates the need for comprehensive learning assistance.

The paid-for-it-twice argument has other problems. Secondary students who complete a college preparatory curriculum vary widely in their mastery of the knowledge and skills. Therefore, students passing enough classes to graduate from high school may still require developmental courses and other forms of noncredit learning assistance in college. Another problem considers the skill level of returning adult college students. Even if they successfully completed college preparatory courses in high school, atrophy of the skills and memory loss over intervening years require their access to learning assistance services (Richardson and King, 1998).

An important event in the history of U.S. higher education occurred in 1890 with creation of the College Board. Its purpose was to establish benchmarks for graduation from high school. The board believed that secondary schools would increase academic rigor through the benchmarks reflected in the Scholastic Aptitude Test. These benchmarks would ensure new college applicants could avoid enrollment in academic preparatory academies. Although the College Board is a powerful influence in education, its quest for eliminating postsecondary learning assistance is unfilled (Boylan, 1988). After a century of intense effort by many stakeholders, nearly 30 percent of all entering college students enroll in one or more developmental courses in English, mathematics, or reading (National Center for Education Statistics, 2003). Many others participate in noncredit learning assistance activities.

Rather than considering budgets for learning assistance programs as expenses, others consider those funds as investments for achieving institutional objectives. A large body of research and evaluation studies clearly demonstrates the impact of learning assistance on increasing student persistence rates toward graduation. Enrollment management organizations such as Noel-Levitz and others recommend implementation of comprehensive learning assistance programs as a part of plans to curtail student dropouts and significantly increase instructional revenues, far in excess of modest investments to maintain or even expand learning assistance programs (McCabe and Day, 1998; Swail, 2004). In addition to building institutional revenues through tuition payments by students persisting to graduation, the number of college dropouts and students with poor job skills have other consequences. Michigan estimated the annual loss to the state economy of $600 million annually because students dropped out of college and failed to develop needed skills for employment in high-demand occupations (Greene, 2000). Similarly, a national study by Phipps (1998) documented the positive impact of learning assistance on the national economy.

## Summary

Postsecondary education grapples with the same issues as the broader society. Who is to be served? At what level of service? Whose responsibility is it for individuals to succeed? Limited resources from state and federal governments intensify debates ongoing for more than a century. Learning assistance is swept into this debate. As Casazza and Bauer (2006) forcefully state, both access and opportunity are essential for achieving the promise of higher education. What are the history forces and experiences from the past that framed today's controversies and issues for learning assistance? The next chapter provides a comprehensive history that provides context for the rest of this report.

# History of Learning Assistance in U.S. Postsecondary Education

EXAMINING THE LONG HISTORY of approaches and programs of learning assistance frames the field and provides context for better understanding of the profession today. This chapter explores phases and forms of learning assistance since the 1600s to today through six distinct phases.

The history of learning assistance begins with the founding of the first college in the United States (Arendale, 2002b). This field has grown in complexity over time. Careful analysis results in the identification of six chronological phases. Names used to describe the field, activities and approaches employed, integration of the field with the core of the institution, and types of students served are compared throughout each phase (Arendale, 2001). Exhibit 1 provides a roadmap for this journey through history.

## Phase One: 1600s to 1820s

The first phase began with the founding of U.S. colleges in the 1600s and concluded in the early 1800s. During that time, learning assistance only provided individual tutors, and no remedial or developmental courses were offered. The majority of students involved in postsecondary education were white males from privileged cultural and economic backgrounds. Tutoring was used in many classes and involved nearly all these affluent students. Therefore, little or no stigma was attached to receiving tutoring services.

### Origins of Learning Assistance

Learning assistance emerged in response to college admission requirements. Admission was denied to nearly all applicants as a result of deficiencies in

**EXHIBIT 1**
**Six Phases of Learning Assistance History**

| Time Phase | Name(s) Commonly Used with Activities | People Served Predominantly During this Time Period |
|---|---|---|
| Phase One: 1600s to 1820s | Tutoring | Privileged white male students |
| Phase Two: 1830s to 1860s | Precollegiate preparatory academy and tutoring | Privileged white male students |
| Phase Three: 1870s to Mid-1940s | Remedial education classes in college preparatory programs and tutoring | Mostly white male students |
| Phase Four: Mid-1940s to 1970s | Compensatory education, counseling center, opportunity program, reading clinic, remedial education classes integrated in the institution, tutoring | Traditional white male students, nontraditional males and females such as war veterans, and federal legislative priority groups: first-generation college students, economically disadvantaged students, and students of color |
| Phase Five: Early 1970s to Mid-1990s | Access program, developmental education, learning assistance, opportunity program, tutoring | Groups listed above, with an increase in older students who return to education or attend postsecondary education for the first time, and some general students who want to deepen mastery of academic content |
| Phase Six: Mid-1990s to the Present | Access program, developmental education, learning assistance, learning/teaching center, learning enrichment, opportunity program | Groups listed above, with an increase in general students, students with disabilities, and faculty members who seek professional development in learning and teaching skills |

*Source:* Arendale, 2001.

foreign language requirements (Latin and Greek) and other academic areas such as mathematics. This situation is not surprising, considering the dismal or nonexistent status of public elementary and secondary education for most citizens at the time.

Students seeking admission to Eaton or Oxford in England sometimes attended a "dame school" to prepare them for the rigorous college admission test. These boarding schools were small tutorial centers run by educated women of high social standing and education. In colonial times, some Virginia aristocratic families sent their children to such schools in England to prepare for college admission tests. Some U.S. clergymen modified this practice by assuming this role and eliminated the need for students to leave the country for academic preparation programs (Gordon and Gordon, 1990).

## *Prevalence of Tutoring Programs*

Precollegiate academic assistance for most students at Harvard and Yale consisted of private tutors who prepared them for college entrance examinations in Greek and Latin and provided evidence of good moral character that was also required for admission. In the mid-1700s, Yale required proficiency in arithmetic in addition to the already stringent requirements. Other postsecondary institutions soon followed. Students who did not attend Latin grammar schools had few options for entering college. One option for gaining admittance to Yale was for a minister to place students in his home for private tutoring until they were ready for the college entrance exam (Cowie, 1936). This option was similar to the dame schools in England.

Once admitted to Harvard, most students continued to receive tutoring, as assigned readings and textbooks were written in Latin. Many college professors delivered lectures in the same language. Even in the most privileged families, verbal and written competency in Latin was unusual. Therefore, Harvard was the first postsecondary institution in the United States to require remedial studies for most of its first-year class of students (Boylan and White, 1987). After admission to prestigious colleges such as Harvard and Yale, students entered a cohort. Each week they met with the same tutor for group sessions. The tutors' primary role was reading aloud the lesson material and then conducting a recitation session to detect whether students had correctly memorized the text. This practice failed to meet the needs for the most gifted and the struggling students, as it focused on the average student's mastery level of the academic content material. The literature contains no evidence of the efficacy of this crude form of academic assistance.

### Impact of Economics

Economics intervened in academic admission policies during the late 1700s. Because of the social norm of considering only white male students from highly prestigious families, most postsecondary institutions found it in their financial interest to admit students less prepared academically but possessing resources to pay college tuition and thus generate more revenue. By the time of the American Revolution, institutions began to differentiate themselves from one another by academic preparation levels of incoming college students and their official mission statements. Amherst and Williams admitted students unable to attend Harvard and Yale as a result of lower academic preparation or inadequate finances (Casazza and Silverman, 1996). Students experienced unofficial segregation policies and procedures. Stereotypes of perceived academic inabilities and discrimination against females and students of color fueled this discrimination. Nathaniel Hawthorne described the students at Williams as "a rough, brown featured, schoolmaster-looking, half-bumpkin, half-scholar, in black, ill-cut broadcloth" (Rudolph, 1956, p. 47). These assumptions, based on ethnic and class prejudices, reflected social norms and prejudices shared by many in society, including key college policymakers. Admission criteria and procedures influenced by these stereotypes contributed to differentiation and stratification among postsecondary institutions.

# Phase Two: 1830s to 1860s

Academic preparation academies emerged during the mid-1800s. These new postsecondary education units provided education equivalent to public high schools, which were not common in most of the United States at the time. Colleges recognized that tutoring as it was being practiced was insufficient to serve the needs of the expanding college student population. Often academies operated in the local community rather than on the college campus. In addition to tutoring, the academies enrolled students in remedial classes in reading, writing, and mathematics. This phase was a short one, as the expansion of public education across the United States replaced the need for many of the new academies. The composition of the student body changed little during this phase. Most students were white males from privileged families. Because most students were involved with learning assistance and from the upper class, little stigma was attached, as it was perceived as a natural part of the education process, a process that was available to so few at the time.

## Impact of Jacksonian Democracy

Some historians identified several elements of Jacksonian democracy as affecting U.S. society in the mid-1800s. Whites benefited from the extension of voting privileges, middle-class workers and small shop owners received financial support, and education was extended to more of the population. One application of Jacksonian democracy was expansion of postsecondary education through common schools, public education, and an expanded curriculum for more people in the middle class rather than only the most privileged.

During this time, expansion of postsecondary education was essential to support development of the economic middle class of merchants, tradesman, engineers, agriculturalists, and scientists needed to meet the needs of the growing nation and to support its economic development. This intersection of interests among political progressives and economic forces indirectly supported learning assistance as a means to ensure higher productivity of colleges to graduate sufficient numbers of skilled workers and leaders.

With poor or nonexistent secondary education and even inadequate primary education in some cases, however, many college aspirants could barely read and write (Craig, 1997). The number of those who tutored and the number who received tutorial assistance were nearly identical to the number of teaching faculty and their enrolled students (Brier, 1984), documenting the extensive involvement of learning assistance in postsecondary education. Since the early years, debate has continued about how to meet the needs of admitted college students. Providing tutoring for students was insufficient to meet their needs during this time. More services would emerge.

One option for meeting students' academic preparation needs was to provide remedial and developmental courses in the institution's curriculum. Proponents of elitism in postsecondary education prevailed temporarily against that option, however. The fixed college curriculum prescribed the same slate of classical courses for all students, without regard to individual needs for development of improved learning strategies and mastery of fundamental academic content material in mathematics and writing. Thus, academic preparatory academies continued to house remedial and developmental courses.

## Academic Preparatory Academies

In 1830, New York University created an early prototype of an academic preparatory academy. It provided instruction in mathematics, physical science, philosophy, and English literature (Dempsey, 1985). The focus, however, was acquiring basic academic content knowledge, not the cognitive learning strategies that are often prerequisite for mastery of new academic material. These academies were a necessary bridge for many college aspirants as a result of the lack of formal secondary education for many. The U.S. education movement started from the top down. First, colleges and universities were established and then public elementary and secondary schools were developed. Some colleges functioned essentially as both high schools and rigorous colleges. The academic preparatory academies supported the rising academic rigor of postsecondary institutions and provided an access conduit for those seeking a college education. The academies expanded with surprising speed in a short time. By 1894, 40 percent of first-year college students had enrolled in college preparatory courses (Ignash, 1997).

Since the beginning, tutorial programs were the most common form of academic enrichment and support at most prestigious institutions such as Harvard and Yale. Many college administrators responded to the high number of students academically underprepared by creating a special academic department that was essential to meet their academic needs. In less selective institutions, the number of underprepared students outnumbered those not requiring additional support. For example, the University of Wisconsin in 1865 could place only forty-one of 331 admitted students in "regular" graduation credit courses. The majority of the new students admitted were restricted to remedial courses (Shedd, 1932). Quality of primary and secondary education was uneven or missing in most of the United States. Most colleges provided instruction in basic skills of spelling, writing, geography, and mathematics, as they were the only venue for such instruction (Brier, 1984). Instruction in basic content areas lengthened the undergraduate bachelor's academic degree to six years or more (Casazza and Silverman, 1996).

In 1849, the University of Wisconsin established the first modern learning assistance program. Instead of offering remedial courses through an external academic preparatory academy, Wisconsin created an academic department for these courses and hired a separate faculty to teach them. The Department of Preparatory Studies instructed students through remedial courses in reading, writing, and arithmetic. Because of an insufficient number of tutors to meet the academic needs of most admitted students, the institution quickly responded by establishing the new academic department. Of the 331 admitted students, 290 enrolled in one or more remedial courses in the preparatory studies department. These courses were similar to those offered at a public high school (Brubacher and Rudy, 1976). Many institutions across the United States implemented the Wisconsin model of learning assistance (Brier, 1984). The department persisted until 1880. Continuous internal political battles among the department, campus administrators, and the rest of the university faculty served as a catalyst for its demise. Faculty members from outside the department demanded its elimination because of the fear of stigma for the university. College administrators tried to appease critics through strategies such as renaming the department. New campus administrators finally closed the department after its short and contentious history (Curti and Carstensen, 1949).

Academic preparatory departments emerged at more than 80 percent of all postsecondary institutions (Canfield, 1889). These departments bridged the gap between inadequate academic preparation of high school graduates and college-level curricular expectations (Clemont, 1899). Review of college admission documents indicated that the farther west the college was located, the lower the entrance requirements for the institution as a result of insufficient preparation in high school. As the public school movement spread from the Northeast farther south and west, college entrance requirements of the institutions eventually rose. After a half century of use, however, remedial college credit courses were entrenched in most colleges.

### Recruitment of Academically Underprepared Students

After the U.S. Civil War, students who were considered academically under-prepared were aggressively recruited. Economic and social changes throughout the United States fueled by the Civil War significantly influenced expansion of learning assistance at more colleges. Many male students did not seek admission or left college to join their respective armies. Many colleges in the North and South replaced them and their tuition payments through expanded academic preparatory departments that supported underage students who were too young to enlist. Examples from the North include Valparaiso University in Indiana, which replaced college students through a rapid expansion of the academic preparatory department. Although the liberal arts college and theology school at Bucknell University closed temporarily in 1865, the academic preparatory school at the same college significantly increased its enrollment. Offsetting enroll-ment decreases saved many institutions from closing. Southern colleges followed the same pattern of Northern institutions through extended academic prepara-tory departments and acceptance of applicants formerly denied admission. In 1861 the University of Alabama created an academic preparatory department for boys twelve years and older. In 1863 the University of Georgia created Uni-versity High School and suspended rules prohibiting admission of boys younger than fourteen to the university. The Faculty Senate of South Carolina College in 1862 voted to admit young students to replace revenue lost by former stu-dents who had left the institution to join the Confederate Army (Rudy, 1996).

# Phase Three: 1870s to Mid-1940s

The third phase of postsecondary education history began during the late 1800s and continued until World War II. The major activities during this era were expansion of tutoring and incorporation of remedial courses in the col-lege curriculum. Academic preparatory academies had been the temporary home for this curriculum earlier in the 1800s. The most frequent service con-tinued to be individual and group tutoring. White male students from privi-leged cultural and economic backgrounds still dominated college campuses. Women and students of color attended newly established institutions reserved for them. These institutions also embraced remedial courses.

## *Relationship of the Federal Government and Learning Assistance*

The federal government increased direct involvement with postsecondary education during this time. The First Morrill Act (1862) established land-grant colleges, which was the federal government's first significant financial involvement with postsecondary education. The mission of these new colleges fostered new degree programs in applied education such as agriculture and the mechanical arts. Established denominational private institutions had not previously offered this curriculum. This action broadened the curriculum and increased access for students of modest academic preparation and lower socioeconomic backgrounds.

Although colleges offered wider access through the 1862 Morrill Act, academic preparation of potential students remained uneven. Many new college students had not attended public high school, as few were in operation in the expanding West of the United States. The dramatic widening of access to postsecondary education accelerated development of academic departments that offered remedial courses and tutoring deemed essential for the new students. "Iowa State College simply required that entering freshman be fourteen years old and able to read, write, and do arithmetic. However, when they lacked these skills, students were placed in the college's preparatory department" (Maxwell, 1997, p. 11). College enrollments soared and many of these new students enrolled in remedial courses. Offering remedial courses and other learning assistance services in a college department addressed many of the problems experienced by external academic preparatory academies such as lack of coordinated curriculum, poor teaching facilities, lack of proper administrative control, and increased stigma for participating students. These problems were the result of the very nature of these academies, as they were clearly separate and seen just as a prerequisite to the college experience.

## *Remedial Education*

The need for academic preparatory departments increased with admission of more students that were academically underprepared. Eighty-four percent of land-grant institutions offered remedial courses by the late 1880s (Craig, 1997). The most frequent term used to describe learning assistance from the 1860s through the early 1960s was "remedial education." Remedial education targeted students' specific skill deficits and employed new educational approaches. Clowes (1980) applied an analogy of the traditional medical model for remedial education. Academic weakness was detected through assessment. The problem was hoped to be cured through prescribed treatment. Clowes categorized students enrolled in remedial education as "academically backward or less able students" (p. 8). Repeated academic treatment persisted until students achieved the desired outcomes or "cures." Students possessed many academic deficits needing prescriptive remediation. Remedial education focused on cognitive deficits and not on improvements in the affective domain. An early glossary developed by the College Reading and Learning Association defined remedial as "instruction designed to remove a student's deficiencies in the basic entry or exit level skills at a prescribed level of proficiency in order to make him/her competitive with peers" (Rubin, 1991, p. 9). Remedial students were identified as "students who are required to participate in specific academic improvement courses/programs as a condition of entry to college" (p. 9).

Remedial education was a prerequisite to enrolling in college-level courses. Remedial courses focused on acquiring skills and knowledge at the secondary school level. Developmental courses, on the other hand, developed skills above the exit level from high school that were needed for success in college. These courses entered the college curriculum during the next historical phase.

In 1879 Harvard admitted 50 percent of applicants "on condition" because they failed the entrance examination. Tutorial programs initially designed for success with college entrance exams were expanded to assist these provisionally admitted students to succeed in their college courses (Weidner, 1990). The Harvard Reports of 1892, 1895, and 1897 documented poor academic preparation of admitted students. University administrators were surprised to discover that students who suffered academic difficulty were not only those from poor or nonexistent high school education. Instead, it was also the "picked boys" (Goodwin, 1895, p. 292), students from the upper class of U.S. society (Hill, 1885). Provision of tutoring and remedial credit courses demonstrated academic rigor at Harvard and exceeded the academic preparation level even for students with formal preparation for postsecondary education. The gap between academic preparation and college performance placed many of the elite students in need of learning assistance (Brier, 1984).

## Remedial Courses in the Curriculum

By 1874 Harvard was first to offer a first-year remedial English course in response to faculty complaints that too many students lacked competency for formal writing activities. Harvard was the first institution that permitted elective courses in response to changing needs of the curriculum. Without flexibility with course options, remedial courses would have been available only as a precollege option. Academic conditions remained unchanged at Harvard, Yale, Princeton, and Columbia by 1907 when half the students failed to earn the minimum composite entrance exam score. Harvard offered a remedial reading course beginning in the early 1900s (Brubacher and Rudy, 1976).

One of the earliest manifestations of college-level learning assistance was the remedial course. The most frequent remedial courses were reading and study skills. More than 350 colleges in 1909 offered "how to study" classes for academically underprepared students. The U.S. Commissioner for Education reported in 1913 that approximately 80 percent of postsecondary institutions offered college preparatory programs with a wide variety of services, including tutoring and remedial courses (Maxwell, 1979). This rate was nearly the same as the mid-1800s. Sensitive to perceptions by students, professors, and others, many colleges began to redefine remedial activities to make them more acceptable by students and campus administrators. When the director of Harvard's Bureau of Study Counsel renamed Remedial Reading to the Reading Class, enrollment increased from thirty to four hundred annually in 1938 (Wyatt, 1992). Through the introduction of the first developmental course, provision of noncredit academic support, and careful use of language to describe its services and course offerings, the learning assistance field owes much to the leadership and innovations of Harvard University.

Junior colleges (later renamed community colleges) extended the new secondary school movement in the early 1900s. Among the broad mission of many junior colleges was college academic preparation. An analogy for this focus on serving academically underprepared students is calling them "the Ellis Island of higher education" (Vaughan, 1983, p. 9). Many four-year institutions transferred their academic preparatory programs to junior colleges in the early 1900s. As described earlier, standardized admissions test scores permitted colleges to refer students to different types of institutions that maintained varying levels of admission selectivity. As four-year institutions received more state and federal appropriations, the institutional financial profile improved. The need to admit high numbers of students who needed academic help to generate tuition revenue and meet institutional expenses lessened (Richardson, Martens, and Fisk, 1981).

A national survey in 1929 of institutions revealed about one-fourth of survey respondents confirmed that their college assessed reading with the admission examination. Nearly half of all students were enrolled in remedial courses (Parr, 1930). These courses often focused heavily on reading skills. Nearly 90 percent of respondents stated they had not conducted research studies regarding the effectiveness of their learning assistance program (Parr, 1930). Societal changes in the middle of the twentieth century required a major expansion of learning assistance to meet a rapidly growing student body—growing in its diversity and level of academic preparation for college-level work.

## Phase Four: Mid-1940s to 1970s

The fourth phase of learning assistance history occurred throughout the middle of the twentieth century. Learning assistance dramatically expanded to meet increased needs resulting from escalating college enrollment. Building on past practices of tutoring and remedial courses, learning assistance expanded services to more students through compensatory education and learning assistance centers. Stigma heightened for learning assistance participants because of increased stratification of academic preparation among entering students. Although previously enrollment in remedial classes was common for most college students (Brubacher and Rudy, 1976; Maxwell, 1979), it was no longer the case. Entering students from privileged backgrounds were better prepared academically than the new first-generation college and economically disadvantaged students who were entering postsecondary education for the first time. Stigma began to attach to the students who enrolled in the remedial and subsequent developmental courses by those who did not need to do so. Well-prepared privileged students did not need extensive learning assistance during college as had the previous generation of college students. The new students, especially those from rural communities and urban centers and many historically underrepresented students of color, had uneven access to such education. This dichotomy of experiences created a perception that developmental courses were needed primarily for students of color. Actually, two-thirds of students enrolled in these courses were white, but it is true that students of color are twice as likely at two-year colleges and three times more likely at four-year institutions to enroll in the courses in relationship to their proportion of the overall population of all college students (Boylan, Bonham, and Bliss, 1994).

## *Increased Federal Involvement*
Federal involvement intensified during this time with increased financial support, legislative oversight, and creation of new college access programs. Significant events occurred: the GI bill, expansion of civil rights, and equal opportunity legislation. The National Center for Education Statistics (1993) tracks a variety of educational activities, including rates of college enrollment. A retrospective in trends over a period of 120 years revealed an increase in college enrollment. College enrollment increased significantly during the 1950s, as the college enrollment rate rose from 15 to 24 percent among eighteen- to twenty-four-year-olds over that decade. During the 1960s, the rate increased to 35 percent, finally reaching 45 percent in the 1970s. Much of this later growth was the result of increased enrollment by adult and part-time students, who required learning assistance support different from their peers (National Center for Education Statistics, 1993).

Colleges were increasingly asked to provide services for older students who often faced concurrent challenges of failure to enroll in college-bound curriculum while in high school and the interruption of education between high school and college as a result of entering the workforce, raising a family, or enlisting in the military. Academic skills often atrophied during the intervening years. These students often brought multiple needs that required academic support and enrichment. Many college preparatory programs expanded as a result. A national survey (Barbe, 1951) documented the growth of reading clinics created to meet the increased number of students academically underprepared for college-level work. Another resource introduced beginning in the 1950s was counseling services in remedial programs (Kulik and Kulik, 1991).

Another catalyst for change was the civil rights movement, manifested in the early 1960s in various forms that resulted in major societal changes of infrastructure—including in learning assistance programs (Chazan, 1973; Clowes, 1980). The Civil Rights Act of 1964 and other programs of President Lyndon Johnson's Great Society focused on increasing opportunities for people of color as well as those people historically excluded from many of society's benefits. Learning assistance services, especially remedial and developmental courses, took on additional tasks. Their responsibility expanded beyond preparation of students for college-level courses, and the learning assistance field received an indirect mandate to serve as a major resource to enable postsecondary institutions to increase dramatically their enrollments by students who had been excluded before—the poor, students of color, and students from families that had never completed college. This informal social responsibility by the learning assistance community would overwhelm its capacity to meet the need as a result of insufficient funding and a lack of trained personnel to provide the services. Although not formally stated in official documents, college learning assistance programs were expected to compensate for inadequate secondary schools, especially in rural and urban centers, and assist students to quickly develop college-level skills in an academic term or two. Overcoming an inadequate elementary and secondary education with limited time, resources, and personnel was a nearly impossible task. The field is still informally held to these expectations today and contributes to criticism for not achieving desired student outcomes.

### Compensatory Education

Deep-rooted social problems influencing many students of color and those from low socioeconomic backgrounds created the need for a new type of education program. During the early 1960s, national civil rights legislation established the Office of Compensatory Education in the U.S. Office of Education (Chazan, 1973). The civil rights movement chose a different perspective of learning assistance. "Compensatory education" remedied a previous state of discrimination: "Compensatory education in higher education would take the form of remediation activities such as preparatory and supplementary work . . . all with a program to provide an enriching experience beyond the academic environment to counterbalance a nonsupportive home environment" (Clowes, 1980, p. 8).

Some believed environmental conditions, often induced by poverty, were responsible for students' poor academic achievement. Compensatory education defined itself as "those efforts designed to make up for the debilitating consequences of discrimination and poverty" (Frost and Rowland, 1971, p. vii). President Johnson's War on Poverty also targeted the negative outcomes caused by these environmental conditions. Compensatory education provided an improved home environment that had been identified as a significant factor for future academic achievement (Maxwell, 1997; Ntuk-Iden, 1978). This paradigm shift from remediating deficits of individual students to remedying deficits of the learning environment and the community required different learning assistance interventions. The response was systemic and involved interventions beyond the provision of tutorial programs and remedial credit courses. Such compensatory programs required significant federal oversight, funding, and management.

New compensatory education programs such as TRIO and other Equal Opportunity programs originated in the 1969 civil rights legislation. According to federal legislation, student eligibility for these new programs required them to meet one or more of the following criteria: (1) neither parent completed college; (2) an economically disadvantaged background; or (3) an eligible disability. The TRIO college access programs became an official entitlement for a federally defined population based on historical underrepresentation in postsecondary education or physical disability (Kerstiens, 1997).

Compensatory education also included traditional approaches to learning assistance—tutoring, counseling, and remedial credit courses—along with a new package of activities including educational enrichment and cultural experiences (Clowes, 1980). Compensatory education leaders distanced themselves from traditional learning assistance activities, however, to avoid the stigma associated with those programs. They positioned compensatory education as creating a new learning culture for students who had suffered historic discrimination and had been underserved by their previous education (Clowes, 1980).

Compensatory education was based on the public health model rather than the medical model (Clowes, 1980). The model expanded beyond the individual to the surrounding academic and economic environment that affected students. Identifying student deficits, providing remedial assistance, and adding supplemental enrichment activities were essential for compensatory education. In addition to a curriculum that included remedial courses, compensatory education also sought to immerse students in a new learning culture that included enrichment activities.

Therefore, compensatory education is not identical to traditional learning assistance approaches. It provides a specific response to a new student population in postsecondary education. Added to its mission was the cultural enrichment of students whose impoverished backgrounds mandated a different approach. Rather than changing the physical surroundings in which students lived and attended school, compensatory education sought to create a separate and enriched learning community for these students. Another approach to create a supportive learning environment for historically underrepresented college students took place in the junior and community colleges.

Federally funded compensatory education programs were a response by the national government to historic injustices. These new programs were accountable, monitored, and funded by the federal government. They were a direct intervention into individual postsecondary institutions. Only approved students could be served through the programs to ensure that the local institution did not divert funds for other purposes. This direct and narrow focus met the needs of many who were served (Grout, 2003). It also became an enormous missed opportunity that not only marginalized the students served and the compensatory programs but also failed to meet the larger issue.

The campus environment and allocation of resources also contributed to lower performance by historically excluded students of color, poor students, and first-generation students. The federal response could have been to hold postsecondary institutions accountable for outcomes of all students. Instead, the response was to create small communities that operated in the larger institutions that could only serve about 10 percent of eligible students (Nealy, 2009; Swail and Roth, 2000). States could also have joined this demand for accountability and made college funding contingent on improved student outcomes, including persistence toward graduation, for not only the overall student population but also for demographic groups such as those from low socioeconomic status, students of color, and first-generation students.

The British provide a model for this type of accountability for higher education. Their "widening participation" initiative holds colleges accountable for student outcomes, among them graduation rates for all students, including those historically neglected (Higher Education Funding Council for England, 2006). Rather than national funds provided for narrowly targeted populations and accompanying services, the funds are for initiatives that result in changes in the campus culture and are critical elements of the campus strategic goals (Higher Education Funding Council for England, 2006). The demographics of the entering student body are to be reflected in the graduating students, or part of the annual appropriation by the national government is subject to withholding. This type of financial accountability as well as supplemental funding from the government for efforts at widening participation could have been implemented in the United States as well.

Instead, the federal government informally endorsed the marginalization of first-generation, economically disadvantaged, and disabled students by providing programs for only a small portion of those who were eligible. These students were identified as different from the others and provided separate programs to serve them, and the participants as well as the service providers suffered from the ensuing stigma while the institutional culture remained essentially unchanged.

## Role of the Junior and Community Colleges

When junior and community colleges expanded in the early 1900s, the entry-level test scores for college applicants were moderately lower than those for four-year institutions (Koos, 1924). This situation dramatically changed in the 1960s as open-door admissions policies at two-year colleges brought many students to postsecondary education that formerly entered the workforce immediately after high school. Junior colleges expanded their mission beyond only preparing students for successful transfer to senior institutions. Community colleges retrained their transfer function and expanded their mission to serve students who were academically underprepared and those enrolled in new certificate vocational programs that served the local community. This shift in focus led the majority of these junior colleges to rename themselves community colleges because of their expanded vision and mission of service (Cohen and Brawer, 2002).

Increased pressure was placed on community colleges in the 1970s and 1980s as four-year institutions recruited more college-bound students to replace ballooning enrollments from returning war veterans (who used the federal GI bill) and the subsequent postwar baby boom. Senior institutions recruited more academically able students and left community colleges to seek more students who were academically underprepared, dramatically increasing the need for comprehensive learning assistance centers and remedial or developmental community college courses. An unanticipated result of this shift in the academic profile of students enrolled at senior institutions created a false perception that little need existed for learning assistance. The opposite occurred at four-year institutions as faculty perceived, wrongly, that new student admits were more academically able to master difficult course material (Hankin, 1996). The gap between student preparation and faculty expectations required a different form of learning assistance, leading to the creation of noncredit learning assistance centers and the decline of remedial credit courses.

New populations of nontraditional students joined traditional-aged students. Expanded federal financial aid through the GI bill and federal civil rights legislation that created compensatory programs such as TRIO fueled an increase in enrollments. The rapidly growing community colleges became the primary offerors of credit-bearing remedial and developmental courses. The core mission of two-year colleges often included providing services for students who had been identified as academically underprepared, but no corresponding statement was made about serving these students in most public four-year colleges and universities. This lack of official institutional priority for serving students that were academically underprepared in one or more academic content areas served as a catalyst for the shift in credit-bearing remedial and developmental offerings from four-year to two-year institutions. This shift contributed to the attachment of further stigma to remedial and developmental courses.

Before this shift occurred in the 1990s, however, many college academic preparatory services at four-year and two-year institutions had responded to the new influx of students by increasing the comprehensiveness of their learning services (Boylan, 1988; Boylan, 1995a). In the mid-1970s, nearly 80 percent of all postsecondary institutions provided academic enrichment and support programs (Roueche and Snow, 1977). Although this rate was nearly the same as the late 1880s, services provided by these programs were more comprehensive, extensive, and coordinated than earlier ones.

Almost half of first-time community college students in the late 1960s and 1970s were underprepared for college-level courses in one or more academic areas. Students often enrolled in one or more developmental courses (Roueche and Roueche, 1999; McCabe and Day, 1998). Although college-bound students in high school enrolled in college preparatory courses, they may have selected the wrong ones or the quality of them may have been insufficient for success in first-year, graduation-credit college courses (Horn, Chen, and MPR Associates, 1998). Frustration with the inability to predict student success created great frustration for all stakeholders involved in the academic enterprise: "The open door often turned into a revolving door, with students dropping out and stopping out regularly. This led to a highly charged debate about the lowering of standards, often followed by the call to raise admission standards and close the doors of opportunity to the thousands of prospective new students" (Casazza and Silverman, 1996, p. 28).

Sometimes change occurs because of intentional choices and visionary leadership by a few individuals. Other times it occurs through reaction to the surrounding environment. Learning assistance during this phase changed because of the latter reason. A major variable that affected U.S. postsecondary education in the mid-1900s was rapid expansion of the student body and failure by many institutions to provide sufficient learning assistance services to support their academic success. As a major influx of new students came into college, the previous learning assistance activities were unable to meet the need. For example, only a fixed number of counseling appointments were available weekly, as few colleges were able or willing to hire more staff. The same was true for faculty teaching remedial courses. Newer, more flexible and scalable learning assistance systems were created. These new services employed student and paraprofessional staff along with the professional staff, prompting creation of new learning assistance approaches in the fifth phase of higher education history.

# Phase Five: 1970s to Mid-1990s

The fifth phase of postsecondary education history introduced new learning assistance non-credit-bearing activities and approaches, especially among public four-year institutions. A second feature of this phase was curtailment of remedial instruction that focused on high school students' development of skills. Corresponding with that decrease, developmental courses that focused on the skill development required for college-level courses rapidly increased. Learning assistance built on past activities of tutoring and credit-bearing courses was replaced by learning assistance centers that served students from a wider range of academic ability.

New forms of learning assistance emerged to serve students with low academic preparation or those who had previously earned low grades in a college course. Previously, nearly all students experienced learning assistance. As the learning assistance model and student body changed, some participated and some did not. The college student body became more diverse with regard to economic, cultural, and academic preparation. Learning assistance grew more quickly at community colleges because they enrolled the largest numbers of underprepared students. Those who participated, especially those forced to participate because of mandatory placement in remedial or developmental courses, were more stigmatized.

### Learning Assistance

In the early 1970s, learning assistance centers (LACs) were introduced (Arendale, 2004; Christ, 1971). Frank Christ at California State University–Long Beach developed the first LAC (then called the learning assistance support system) and was the first to use the technical term in the professional literature (Arendale, 2004). White and Schnuth (1990) identified a distinguishing characteristic of LACs: their comprehensive nature and mission in the institution. Rather than an exclusive focus on underprepared students, LACs extended services for all students and even faculty members. The center naturally extended the classroom with enrichment activities for all students.

LACs, according to Christ, were comprehensive in their theoretical underpinnings and services provided, compared with earlier reading labs and other forms of academic assistance. LACs shared a common mission: to meet the needs of students facing academic difficulty in a course and to provide supplemental and enrichment learning opportunities for any students at the institution. The reading labs worked only for students dealing with severe difficulty in reading. Students went to counseling centers only when they were having extreme academic and emotional difficulties. The LACs served these students and the general student population as well. Therefore, no stigma was attached to the LACs. "[LACs] differed significantly from previous academic support services by introducing concepts and strategies from human development, the psychology of learning, educational technology, and corporate management into an operational rationale specific to higher education; by functioning as a campus-wide support system in a centralized operational facility; by vigorously opposing any stigma that it was 'remedial' and only for inadequately prepared, provisionally admitted, or probationary students; and by emphasizing 'management by objectives' and a cybernetic subsystem of ongoing evaluation to elicit and use feedback from users for constant program modification" (Christ, 1997, pp. 1–2). Learning centers avoided the remedial label that had stigmatized other forms of learning assistance. Although some institutions did not offer developmental courses, especially public four-year institutions, nearly all institutions accepted the challenge to offer learning assistance and enrichment services to all students.

Various factors encouraged the rapid development of learning centers, which (1) applied technology for individualized learning; (2) responded to lowered admission standards; (3) focused on cognitive learning strategies; (4) increased student retention; and (5) were perceived to enrich learning for all students, regardless of their previous level of academic performance (Enright, 1975). The LAC was a catalyst for improved learning across the campus. Rather than continuing the previous practice of preparatory programs and remedial courses that were often outside the heart of the college, these centers contributed to the core institutional mission (Hultgren, 1970; Kerstiens, 1972). Faculty members often recognized these centers as extensions of the classroom and encouraged their use for deeper mastery of college-level material. "The resource center does not define the goals of the learning it supports; it accepts the goals of the faculty and the students" (Henderson, Melloni, and Sherman, 1971, p. 5). LACs were consolidated, and centralized operations were housed in a single location on campus. All students—not just those experiencing academic difficulty—benefited from a LAC's services. LACs provided a model for learning and teaching centers established at some U.S. colleges beginning in the 1980s that assisted students and faculty members. Those centers supported students' mastery of rigorous academic content material and faculty professional development.

As mentioned, LACs were sometimes integrated into campuswide student retention initiatives. Organizations such as the Noel-Levitz centers have acknowledged a variety of learning assistance programs by recognizing increased student persistence (Noel-Levitz Center, 2010). A LAC that includes this objective as part of its mission is at Lees-McRae College (Banner Elk, North Carolina). The Division of Student Success (http://www.lmc.edu/sites/Acaemics/StudentSuccess/) hosts traditional learning assistance services. It also provides additional services supporting student retention by housing the Office of Students with Disabilities, the First Year Experience Program, summer orientation, and student retention services for students placed on academic probation. Learning assistance is bundled with other campus services and guided by the campus student retention plan. Sometimes these bundled efforts also support persistence in college majors in academically challenging areas such as science, technology, engineering, and mathematics (Seymour and Hewitt, 1997).

### Developmental Education
Beginning in the 1970s, "developmental education" emerged as another term used to describe the field of learning assistance. This term borrowed concepts from the field of college student personnel. An underlying assumption was that all college students were developing throughout their college career. "The notion of developmental sequence is the kingpin of developmental theory. . . . A goal of education is to stimulate the individual to move to the next stage in the sequence" (Cross, 1976, p. 158). This perspective returned learning assistance to its historic roots by focusing on the entire student population.

Proponents of developmental education viewed it as a more comprehensive model because it focused on personal development of the academic and affective domains (Boylan, 1995b; Casazza and Silverman, 1996; Hashway, 1988; Higbee, 2005; Higbee and Dwinell, 1998). This value-added or talent development perspective assumed each student possessed skills or knowledge that could be further developed. Cross expressed the differences between remedial and developmental education in the following way: "If the purpose of the program is to overcome academic deficiencies, I would term the program remedial, in the standard dictionary sense in which remediation is concerned with correcting weaknesses. If, however, the purpose of the program is to develop the diverse talents of students, whether academic or not, I would term the program developmental. Its mission is to give attention to the fullest possible development of talent and to develop strengths as well as to correct weaknesses" (Cross, 1976, p. 31).

## Access Programs

Thus far this review of learning assistance has focused on its use in the United States. Tutorial programs and the earlier dame schools were common learning assistance approaches in Europe. During this period, the United Kingdom developed a new approach for learning assistance called "access programs."

Unlike the system in the United States, higher education in most other countries was coordinated, funded, and evaluated by the national government. The United Kingdom employed a different approach and terminology to meet the needs of students who were academically underprepared during the late 1970s. Two organizations in particular provided leadership—the European Access Network (http://www.ean-edu.org/) and the Institute for Access Studies (http://www.staffs.ac.uk/institutes/access/). Most postsecondary institutions in the United Kingdom offered student services similar to those in the United States, including advising, counseling, disability services, orientation, mentoring, and tutoring (Thomas, Quinn, Slack, and Casey, 2003). Students with additional needs for developmental courses were required to complete a perquisite certificate offered through the access program.

One noticeable difference between the United States and the United Kingdom was length of academic terms of remedial or developmental courses.

The United Kingdom organized these courses into a unit called an "access program." These programs were located in a postsecondary institution or an adult education center operated independently in the local community. Admission to a college or university depended on successful completion of the one-year program, which also resulted in a certificate of completion. Although some similarities existed between access programs in the United Kingdom and academic preparatory programs in the United States, an important difference between the two countries was that U.S. colleges were more likely to admit students who had less academic preparation than were those in the United Kingdom. U.S. institutions were more willing to admit students to determine whether they could benefit from the college experience, while U.K. institutions demanded a greater likelihood of academic success before admission (Burke, 2002; Fulton and others, 1981).

The U.K. national government first initiated access programs in 1978. In addition to the proactive stance by the national government to require this prerequisite learning venue for some college aspirants, several distinctive features of access programs contrasted with learning assistance in the United States:

They were recognized as an official route into further higher education.

They met minimum standards set by the national government before access programs students were admitted to college.

They targeted underrepresented students such as disabled learners, the unemployed, female returnees, minority ethnic groups, and those from lower socioeconomic backgrounds.

They were evaluated by the Quality Assurance Agency, a national government agency similar to the U.S. Government Accounting Office (Universities and Colleges Admission Service, 2003a, 2003b).

The British government created and provides ongoing evaluation for access programs, while in the United States they are generally under local institutional review. In the United States, the federal government is not a partner with learning assistance except for some competitive funds allocated through grant programs such as Title III, Title VI, and TRIO. It has been a missed opportunity for the national learning assistance professional associations to develop a formal, ongoing relationship with the U.S. Department of Education that could have led to more legitimacy, improvement, and perhaps more funding support.

## Pilot Experiments with Outsourcing Developmental Courses

Forces coincided during the late 1980s through the 1990s to experiment with commercial companies' provision of developmental college courses. Nationwide, budget priorities shifted during the 1980s as state revenues previously devoted to public higher education began to erode because of escalating costs for state health care, transportation systems, prison facilities, and public K–12 education. With stagnant revenue growth and escalating operating costs, many colleges identified cost savings perceived to have little negative impact. A popular approach was outsourcing services traditionally performed by college staff. Requiring highly competitive service bids and shifting escalating health insurance and other benefits (the fastest-growing component of labor costs) to subcontractors would save significant costs for institutions. Numerous services were successfully outsourced: bookstores, food service, building maintenance, housing, and transportation services (Lyall and Sell, 2006). Another area for outsourcing was the delivery of developmental courses (Johnsrud, 2000).

A small handful of colleges contracted with Kaplan, Inc. (http://kaplan.com) and Sylvan Learning Systems (http://reportcard.sylvan.info/) in the mid-1990s to provide instruction in remedial and developmental mathematics, reading, and writing. Colleges that participated in the pilot program included Greenville Technical College (South Carolina), Columbia College Chicago (Illinois), Howard Community College and Towson University (Maryland), and several other unnamed proprietary schools. National interest and debate were generated through the pilot projects (Blumenstyk, 2006; Gose, 1997). Initial reports were mixed in Maryland's pilot program with Sylvan (Maryland Higher Education Commission, 1997). Students paid a surcharge between two and four times the regular tuition rate to cover instructional and administrative expenses and allow the companies to turn a profit.

Both Kaplan and Sylvan ended the pilot programs in agreement with the hosting institutions in the late 1990s. The reasons for their failure were primarily economic. The initial hope was to contain instructional costs and deliver improved student achievement and subsequent higher student retention rates that would justify the annual contract cost, but it was unrealistic for a for-profit company to market a program for a lower cost than the ones that could be provided by the institution with the use of modestly paid adjunct instructors who could be assigned large classes (Blumenstyk, 2006; Boylan, 2002a). The same economic forces that were the catalyst for the experiment ultimately became the cause for this first wave of outsourcing to end. A second wave of outsourcing was expected to be more effective during the first decade of the twenty-first century as the focus changed from onsite developmental courses to online tutoring.

### Rise of the Professional Associations

The 1980s witnessed the birth of several national associations serving professionals in the field of learning assistance, coinciding with the explosive growth in college enrollment and number of public postsecondary institutions, especially community colleges. Institutions expanded their teaching staff for remedial and developmental courses. The exponential growth of learning assistance centers required a new category of college employees. These new professionals needed organizations that met needs for postsecondary education rather than older organizations devoted to serving educators in elementary and secondary education. They needed to increase their professionalism and provide venues for conversation with colleagues and experienced leaders in learning assistance. The new organizations provided a supportive community for new professionals who might be isolated on campus and were sometimes stigmatized because of their association with learning assistance programs.

Established in 1952, the Southwest Reading Conference, later renamed the National Reading Conference, was first to serve postsecondary educators in this field. The College Reading and Learning Association (CRLA, previously named the Western College Reading Association and later the Western College Reading and Learning Association) was founded in 1966. The CRLA publishes a quarterly newsletter, annual conference proceedings, and the biannual *Journal of College Reading and Learning*. Conferences are held annually at national venues and at CRLA-affiliated chapters throughout the United States. The focus of the CRLA was clearly postsecondary education. Previously, learning assistance personnel had few options for professional development other than from other organizations with a predominately elementary and secondary education focus such as the International Reading Association. The CRLA and the other learning assistance associations that followed it provided an identity and a place for postsecondary learning assistance professionals to gather and exchange information.

Following passage of national legislation creating the federal TRIO programs for first-generation and economically disadvantaged students, political advocacy was essential to expand financial and stable support for these programs. During the early 1970s, regional professional associations created by TRIO staff members represented their interests for increased national funding and provided professional development services for themselves. Clark Chipman, a regional USDOE higher education administrator for the Upper Midwest, was a key leader for development of the first TRIO association. It was called the Mid-American Association for Educational Opportunity Program Personnel. Afterwards, nine additional regional associations formed across the United States. In 1981 Clark Chipman and Arnold Mitchem coordinated efforts of preceding regional associations to influence national policy through creation of the National Council of Educational Opportunity Associations. In 1988 the association changed its name to the Council on Opportunity in Education (Grout, 2003).

The National Association for Developmental Education (NADE, initially named the National Association for Remedial/Developmental Studies in Post-secondary Education) was founded in 1976. Because of uncertainty about what would become the more widely adopted term, both "remedial" and "developmental" were included in the association's original name. In 1981 the NADE contracted with the National Center for Developmental Education to provide the *Journal of Developmental Education* as a membership benefit and official journal of the association. The NARDSPE changed its name to the NADE in 1984.

A variety of other professional associations were born in the 1990s. The National College Learning Center Association provided professional development for learning center directors. The National Tutoring Association served educators from higher education, secondary education, and private individuals engaged in tutoring. The Association for the Tutoring Profession was created for similar purposes. The Council for Learning Assistance and Developmental Education Associations (initially named the American Council of Developmental Education Associations) began in 1996 to serve as a forum for these professional associations to meet and engage in cooperative activities, information sharing, and networking.

The growth of these organizations signified historically that learning assistance was becoming more complex, employing more professionals, and needed professional associations focused on their special needs in higher education. Large established organizations such as the International Reading Association, Conference on College Composition and Communication, and American Mathematical Society generally provided special interest groups for postsecondary learning assistance professionals. They missed the opportunity, however, to fully meet the needs of the professionals who preferred the smaller and more narrowly focused learning assistance associations. This situation led to duplication of services among the larger content-focused organizations and the smaller learning assistance associations. It also may have led to increased stigma for the learning assistance professionals, as they did not become members and attend the conferences of the larger organizations that attracted membership of mainstream college faculty and staff members. It was another way that some learning assistance professionals stood apart from the mainstream in higher education.

### *Support Systems for Leaders and Practitioners*

Several other national organizations, graduate education programs, and publications have contributed to the history of the learning assistance community. A three-year grant from the Kellogg Foundation established the National Center for Developmental Education (NCDE) in 1976. Two years later NCDE began publishing *The Journal of Developmental Education* (initially named *Journal of Developmental and Remedial Education*). *Review of Research in Developmental Education* was another NCDE publication; created in 1983, it focused on current research in the field. Since 1980 the center has also hosted the Kellogg Institute for the Training and Certification of Developmental Educators.

During this period, a variety of formal and informal systems of professional development for learning assistance were established. Practitioners in the field previously relied on degree programs for elementary and secondary education. Secondary educators teaching reading, English, and mathematics staffed many of the learning assistance centers and taught developmental courses in post-secondary institutions.

New graduate programs also emerged to equip learning center professionals at the college level rather than relying on preparation for secondary schools. The first graduate programs in developmental education (M.A. and Ed.S.) began at Appalachian State University in 1972. Grambling State University (Louisiana) in 1986 offered the nation's first doctoral program (Ed.D.). National Louis University (Chicago), Texas State University at San Marcos, and the University of Minnesota–Twin Cities (Minneapolis) also established learning assistance graduate certificate or degree programs during this period. Collectively these advanced degrees contributed to the professionalization and ability to meet student needs by learning assistance faculty and staff members. A major challenge with the national impact of these programs is that they are few in number and many current learning assistance professionals find it difficult to relocate them to meet residency requirements and to secure funds for tuition. An expansion of distance learning pedagogies for the degree programs would permit easier access for graduate students who are place bound and unable to participate in long required residency stays at the degree-granting institutions.

# Phase Six: Mid-1990s to the Present

Turbulence in postsecondary education defines the current phase of history. Learning assistance activities and services have been curtailed at a growing number of four-year institutions, especially large public universities. This change is concurrent with increased diversity of the student population, increased college enrollments, increased competition for institutional funds, and decreased percentage of operating funds from state governments for public institutions. Although the need for learning assistance has expanded, its resources have become scarcer.

In the late 1990s, the perception of learning assistance changed for some— and not for the better. Critics have been particularly harsh toward programs that used the term "developmental education" to describe themselves. Large, public four-year institutions are engaged in intense dialogue about this topic. The terms *developmental education, compensatory education,* and *remedial education* suffer from stigma. In 1998 Martha Maxwell noted, "Developmental education has become a euphemism for remedial with all the negative connotations that word implies. . . . Today, students taking developmental courses are stigmatized. . . In primary and secondary schools the term developmental education applies to programs for the mentally retarded" (Piper, 1998, p. 35). As remedial education engendered negative reactions from some policymakers, so did developmental education.

Several publications have prompted considerable conversation about improving the campus learning environment (Barr and Tagg, 1995; Lazerson, Wagener, and Shumanis, 2000). A number of learning assistance professionals have reinvented themselves as resources for the entire campus—students and faculty alike—by aligning with this paradigm of learning.

A result of the paradigm shift from teaching to learning led to creation of learning and teaching centers at some institutions. Although the name of these centers was the same, two variations were apparent. One type of learning and teaching center provides professional development for the teaching staff. Services include resource libraries, training programs for new instructors, ongoing mentoring programs, classroom observations with subsequent private consultations, and the like. A second type of learning and teaching center extends the professional development services for faculty by providing learning assistance services for students such as tutoring, learning skill workshops, drop-in learning centers, and credit courses.

Methods for operating these teaching and learning centers vary widely. An online search for these centers suggests that most were established at four-year institutions (Center for Teaching Excellence, 2009). Reviewing the Web sites for the centers suggests that they have been expressed differently based on administrative location under academic or student affairs. Those in student affairs tend to have a higher focus on delivery of learning assistance services for students. Those located under academic affairs more commonly focus on teaching faculty development activities. Another factor that has affected these centers is whether a faculty or staff member leads it. Those led by faculty members tend to be under academic affairs, those led by staff members most often under student affairs. Unlike the aforementioned learning assistance professional associations, no clear national organization represents these teaching and learning centers.

The teaching and learning center model has emerged to meet the broad needs that exist to assist student learning and faculty development. An online search for postsecondary teaching and learning centers identified several examples among prestigious institutions. Cornell University (Ithaca, New York), through its Center for Learning and Teaching (http://www.clt.cornell.edu), serves students through the learning strategies center (tutoring, workshops, supplemental classes), student disability services, and international teaching assistance development program (workshops to improve communication and pedagogical skills). Instructors can access teaching assistance services (individual consultations and workshops to improve teaching skills) and faculty services (individual consultations to improve teaching effectiveness). At Stanford University (Palo Alto, California), the Center for Teaching and Learning (http://ctl.stanford.edu/) provides faculty development opportunities and tutoring, learning skills workshops, and academic coaching for students.

As these examples illustrate, common practices of these expanded centers include providing academic assistance to all students enrolled in identified courses, publishing teaching effectiveness newsletters, conducting learning effectiveness workshops, providing teaching mentors, and consulting on innovative instructional delivery. Both illustrate how learning assistance appears very differently at these prestigious institutions in comparison with open access community colleges. Developmental courses are not provided at these institutions; instead, services for students focus on tutoring and noncredit learning strategies workshops.

## Summary

Learning assistance serves a pivotal role in the history of U.S. postsecondary education. It developed a variety of approaches, and the language used to describe it has evolved. Regardless of the expressions, learning assistance bridges the gap between students' academic preparation and expectations of college courses. It began as an embedded service by providing tutoring for all students enrolled in college during the first century of the United States. Later, the services became less embedded in the curriculum—with some students participating in learning assistance and others not. At times it has been essential for supporting student enrollment and persistence to graduation, and at other times it has been rejected and stigmatized. Sometimes these different perspectives on learning assistance have existed at the same time in different types of postsecondary institutions.

As learning assistance approaches permitted voluntary participation or required mandatory placement, stigma sometimes emerged for those using the services. The student body can become divided: students required to participate, students choosing to participate, and those who elect not to participate. The stigma issue is most pronounced for students enrolled in remedial or developmental credit courses, but credit courses are only one approach to learning assistance. Other students who did not enroll in such courses often accessed other forms of learning assistance such as tutoring, learning assistance centers, or other services. Students who use these services, however, especially those from more advantaged backgrounds, do not suffer from the same stigma. These learning assistance activities and services are perceived as supplemental or enrichment and have escaped negative stereotyping.

A balanced review of the history places learning assistance in its proper position, operating at the crossroads of three major components of higher education: academic affairs, student affairs, and enrollment management. The next chapter explores the scope and expression of learning assistance today. The expression of learning assistance is often quite different among different institutional types based on admissions selectivity and degrees conferred.

# The Current Nature and Scope of Learning Assistance

POSTSECONDARY EDUCATION VARIES GREATLY with its expression among institutions through admission policies, curriculum design, learning systems, and student expectations. The variability of U.S. education reflects local governance with different regulations from state and national government. Autonomy and local control explain the highly varied expression of learning assistance on college campuses. This chapter explores learning assistance as it operates today.

## Annual Scope of Learning Assistance

It is difficult to estimate the total number of college students who use learning assistance annually. Depending on the institution, learning assistance activities may include enrolling in remedial or developmental credit-bearing courses as well as attending noncredit activities such as tutoring, using learning assistance center resources, or attending a study strategies workshop. Because this chapter focuses on contemporary uses of learning assistance, it emphasizes students who are academically underprepared in one or more academic content areas. This report, however, also includes case studies of learning assistance use by students who do not fit that profile. These students have used it to enrich their learning and support them with rigorous coursework in graduate and professional schools. These enrichment and noncredit learning assistance services expand the number of students participating beyond the one-third of all entering college students enrolling in a developmental course (National Center for Education Statistics, 2003). Rather than counting the number of noncredit users of learning assistance services such as learning assistance centers and tutoring, the national studies report the high percentage of institutions that offer these services (National Center for Education Statistics, 2003). As described earlier, the reasons for the use of learning assistance become more complicated when the same student accesses learning assistance in one class because of academic difficulty, uses a different set of learning assistance services in another to supplement his or her learning, and uses none in other courses during the same or subsequent academic terms. As stated earlier, the use of learning assistance is based on the need presented by the academic course and not necessarily an attribute of overall academic weakness by the individual student.

Some institutions enroll a high percentage of students who are academically underprepared in one or more academic content areas yet graduate them at high rates. The Community College of Denver, through the Center for Educational Advancement (http://www.ccd.edu/LAA/LAAcea.html), provides a comprehensive array of learning assistance services. Accurate assessment and course placement are essential, as most students enroll in one or more developmental courses. Compared with other Colorado community colleges, this institution has the highest number and percentage of students enrolling in these courses. Students completing these required developmental courses graduate at a higher rate from college than students who were admitted and advised not to enroll in developmental courses. Comprehensive learning assistance services enable the institution to broaden access for students with a wider range of academic skills and achieve a high rate of timely graduation for all.

Understanding the scope of learning assistance throughout the United States requires careful review of national studies of enrollment patterns in developmental courses, participation in noncredit activities, and institutional and state policies affecting learning assistance activities. Table 1 focuses on one element of learning assistance, developmental courses in reading, mathematics, or writing. No uniform state or national reporting systems exist for noncredit services such as tutoring and attendance in learning centers (explored later in this report). The terms "remedial" and "developmental" course are used interchangeably in this section.

# TABLE 1
## Comparison of National Data About Learning Assistance: Fall 2000, 1995, 1989, 1983

| Learning Assistance–Related Activity or Policy | 2000[a] | 1995[b] | 1989[c] | 1983 |
|---|---|---|---|---|
| Institution offers noncredit learning assistance service | | | | |
| a. Institution offered at least one type of noncredit learning assistance | n/a | n/a | 98% | 90%[f] |
| b. Institution offered peer tutoring | n/a | n/a | 85% | 84–88%[e] |
| c. Institution offered counseling | n/a | n/a | 82% | 52–56%[e] |
| d. Institution offered learning center | n/a | n/a | 69% | n/a |
| Institution offers at least one developmental course | | | | |
| a. All institutions | 76% | 77% | 74% | 82%[c] |
| b. All public institutions | n/a | n/a | 91% | 94%[c] |
| c. Public two-year institutions | 98% | 100% | n/a | 92–96%[e,g] |
| d. Public four-year institutions | 80% | 80% | n/a | 88–94%[e,g] |
| e. All private institutions | n/a | n/a | 58% | 70%[c] |
| f. Private two-year institutions | 63% | 64% | n/a | 79–89%[e,g] |
| g. Private four-year institutions | 59% | 62% | n/a | 78–90%[e,g] |
| h. All institutions with high percentage of students of color | n/a | 94% | 94% | n/a |
| i. All institutions with high percentage of students who were white | n/a | 76% | 74% | n/a |
| First-year students who enrolled in one or more developmental courses | | | | |
| a. Institutions of all types | 28% | 29% | 30% | 25%[f] |
| b. All public institutions | n/a | n/a | 36% | 27%[f] |
| c. Public two-year institutions | 42% | 41% | n/a | n/a |
| d. Public four-year institutions | 24% | 26% | n/a | n/a |
| e. All private institutions | n/a | n/a | 24% | 15%[f] |
| f. Private two-year institutions | 20% | 22% | n/a | n/a |

(Continued)

**TABLE 1 (Continued)**

| Learning Assistance–Related Activity or Policy | 2000[a] | 1995[b] | 1989[c] | 1983 |
|---|---|---|---|---|
| g. Private four-year institutions | 12% | 13% | n/a | n/a |
| h. Institutions with predominately students of color | n/a | 43% | 55% | n/a |
| i. Institutions with predominately white students | n/a | 26% | 27% | n/a |
| j. Number of students enrolled in one or more developmental courses | 679,840[d] | 629,070[d] | 702,300[d] | 611,000[d] |
| Students at all institutions who successfully completed developmental courses | n/a | 74–77%[e] | 67–77%[e] | 68–74%[e,f] |
| Institution has mandatory course placement testing | 57–61%[e] | 58–64%[e] | n/a | 79%[g] |
| Institution requires enrollment in developmental course based on placement test score | 75–82%[e] | 71–79%[e] | 54–68%[e] | 51–64%[e,f] |
| Transcript credit at all institutions for enrollment in developmental courses | | | | |
| a. Institutional credit | 73–78%[e] | 68–72%[e] | 66–69%[e] | 52–54%[e,f] |
| b. Graduation credit | 10–14%[e] | 15–17%[e] | 15–19%[e] | 23–25%[e,f] |
| Institution offers developmental courses or workshops to local businesses | 21% | 19% | n/a | n/a |
| Institution has time limit for taking developmental courses | 26% | 26% | n/a | n/a |
| Enrollment patterns for students in developmental courses | | | | |
| a. Enrolled more students than before | n/a | 39% | n/a | 63%[f] |
| b. Enrolled fewer students than before | n/a | 14% | n/a | 4%[f] |
| c. Enrolled about the same percentage of students as before | n/a | 47% | n/a | 33%[f] |

*Notes:*
[a]National Center for Education Statistics, 2003.
[b]National Center for Education Statistics, 1996.
[c]National Center for Education Statistics, 1991.
[d]Data calculated by multiplying total number of first-year students by estimated percentage enrolled in one or more developmental courses.
[e]Column entries that display a range represent a mean percentage each for reading, mathematics, and writing.
[f]Wright and Cahalan, 1985.
[g]Lederman, Ryzewic, and Ribaudo, 1983.

Data for Table 1 draw primarily from the National Center for Education Statistics of the U.S. Department of Education (National Center for Education Statistics, 1991, 1996, 2003) during 1989, 1995, and 2000. Data for 1983 come from a variety of sources: National Center for Education Statistics (1985), National Center for Education Statistics data accessed by independent researchers (Wright and Cahalan, 1985), and data collected by the City University of New York (Lederman, Ryzewic, and Ribaudo, 1983). Different reporting procedures among these studies result in some data not collected or reported. In this case, "n/a" appears in the corresponding cell.

Table 1 reveals that learning assistance often expresses itself differently among various institutional types: two-year and four-year, public and private. The services also appear differently in these categories among institutions of differing admissions selectivity. Although noncredit services such as tutoring and learning centers are commonly found among institutions, the provision of developmental courses is more commonly found at two-year institutions. Many institutions, however, provide both credit and noncredit services.

Many students who enroll in postsecondary education participate in learning assistance activities in one form or another. Boylan (1999) confirms that nearly 2 million of the 12 million students enrolling in U.S. postsecondary education enroll in a developmental course or participate in other noncredit services such as tutoring or use of a learning center. Because 600,000 to 700,000 students enroll in the courses, more than 1 million students access noncredit services such as tutoring and learning assistance centers (Boylan, 1999; National Center for Education Statistics, 2003). For the past twenty years, nearly three-quarters of higher education institutions enrolling first-year students have offered at least one developmental reading, writing, or mathematics course. Although four-year research institutions decreased course offerings in this area during the 1990s (Barefoot, 2003), most institutions showed little overall significant change (National Center for Education Statistics, 1991, 1996, 2003). Offerings vary widely among institutional types. The highest percentage offering such courses are public two-year colleges (98 percent), followed by public four-year (80 percent), private two-year (63 percent), and private four-year (59 percent) (National Center for Education Statistics, 2003).

More selective admissions among these categories reduces the likelihood the institution offered such courses (Barefoot, 2003).

About 30 percent of first-time, first-year students enrolled in one or more developmental reading, writing, or mathematics courses since the 1980s. This rate rises to 40 percent of students who are the first in their family to attend college (National Center for Education Statistics, 2003, 2005). For the past two decades, 600,000 to 700,000 first-year students enrolled annually in such courses. As a result of the research protocols used by the federal government for these studies, the data do not include sophomores, juniors, seniors, or graduate students who enroll in remedial or developmental courses; students who participate in noncredit academic enrichment activities such as tutoring, group study review groups, learning strategy workshops, or similar activities; and students of any classification who enroll in remedial or developmental courses in science or study strategies. Therefore, it is reasonable to estimate the number of students accessing credit and noncredit services at 2 million annually (Boylan, 1999).

The following finding comes from the U.S. Department of Education's study focusing primarily on developmental courses (National Center for Education Statistics, 2003). Of students enrolling in these courses, three-quarters successfully complete them. Most students enroll in developmental courses during only one academic term. Students are twice as likely to enroll in the courses at two-year institutions than in four-year colleges and universities. About three-quarters of institutions offer only institutional credit for the courses, while others offer graduation credit. In these cases, the credit counts as a free elective. About three-quarters of institutions require students to enroll in remedial or developmental courses based on their entry-level test scores. This percentage has increased during the 1990s. About two-thirds of institutions restrict concurrent enrollment in graduation-credit courses and developmental courses. Nearly a quarter of institutions establish a time limit for successfully completing these courses. A traditional academic unit such as the English or mathematics department is the most frequent provider of developmental courses, with a separate developmental department following in frequency. Learning centers are less frequently used, though the percentage has grown.

About 20 percent of institutions provide developmental courses and noncredit workshops for local business and industry. Two-year institutions are ten times more likely to offer these services than their four-year counterparts (National Center for Education Statistics, 2003). About 50 percent of two-year colleges offer these services, compared with only about 5 percent of other types of institutions. Of the institutions that provide services to local business and industry, the most popular are in mathematics, followed by reading and writing (National Center for Education Statistics, 2003). Although course objectives and content are similar, these courses are repackaged for the business community, when they are often called professional development and job readiness workshops. For example, a Fundamentals of English course might be called a business communications workshop, and a Fundamentals of Reading course might be repackaged as power reading. Commonly these workshops and courses are offered at the business site (89 percent) and to a lesser extent on the institution's campus (74 percent) (National Center for Education Statistics, 1985, 1991, 1996, 2003; Lederman, Ryzewic, and Ribaudo, 1983; Wright and Cahalan, 1985).

## Cost Estimates for Providing Learning Assistance

It is clear that a large percentage of students use learning assistance services every year. Some policymakers perceive this high volume of participation and wide range of activities as too expensive. Recent studies disprove this view. As pervasive as learning assistance has become, it consumes a minor amount of a given institution's budget. The most recent national study (Phipps, 1998) estimates its cost at less than $1 billion of $115 billion in the public higher education annual budget. This amount includes spending on developmental credit courses and noncredit services (tutoring, drop-in learning centers) that a wide variety of students of varying academic preparation levels use. Saxon and Boylan (2001) confirmed this finding through analysis of other similar studies. Additional analysis by Phipps (1998) found the unit cost of remedial or developmental courses was less than other academic content areas such as English, mathematics, or business. Classes were smaller than for most core academic subjects but cost less. It may be because faculty members who teach developmental courses are paid less compared with faculty members who teach other courses. It may also reflect the heavy use of adjunct and part-time instructors for these courses at public two-year institutions, the primary providers of these courses (National Center for Education Statistics, 2003).

Others advocates (Phipps, 1998; McCabe and Day, 1998; Wilson and Justiz, 1988) argue learning assistance is essential for economic reasons because of the costs to society and the economic level of students who do not complete their college degrees because sufficient learning assistance was lacking. The United States risks development of "an educational and economic underclass whose contributions to society will be limited and whose dependency on others will grow. The risk increases for creating a culture and economy that ignores the talents of a large number of citizens" (Wilson and Justiz, 1988, pp. 9–10). McCabe and Day (1998) estimate that 2 million students each year will drop out of postsecondary education because they did not participate in learning assistance, which will negatively affect their own lives as well as the national economy. Alphen (2009) conducted a multicountry study of the impact of not completing an undergraduate college degree. Controlling for country-level variables, the findings confirmed the negative economic impact of people not obtaining at least an undergraduate degree compared with the cost of providing postsecondary education.

Funded by the Lumina and Wal-Mart foundations, a national study investigated the costs and returns of providing academic support programs and the net impact on revenue at the institution. Institutions were two-year and four-year, public and private, of various sizes, and geographically dispersed throughout the United States. The study found that learning assistance was positively related to higher student persistence and increased revenue above the cost of providing academic support services (Delta Project, 2009). Another study focused on the Community College of Denver concerned the cost-effectiveness of learning assistance. Net revenue generated through higher rates of student persistence were significantly higher than the cost of the learning assistance services (Corash and Baker, 2009).

## Approaches to and Systems of Learning Assistance

Learning assistance encompasses a variety of activities and models with varying levels of efficacy for institutions and participating students. The variety of these models is a result of different policies, funding formulas, student population characteristics, historical traditions, campus culture, political decisions, and stakeholders' expectations.

So far in this chapter, the narrative overview and the statistics aggregate many learning assistance approaches and systems. Better understanding of the choices taken when offering learning assistance occurs when it is categorized into different approaches taken at the institutional level. The three broad categories in Exhibit 2 are based on where and when the particular learning assistance activity is offered: a prerequisite activity on the college campus before a student enrolls in a class for graduation credit; concurrent activity on the college campus while a student is enrolled in a class predicted to be academically challenging; and outsourcing of the learning assistance activity to another institution or commercial firm.

The goal of these three approaches is preparation of students for academic success in a rigorous core curriculum of college-level course that exceeds the average of other college-level classes and is challenging for many members of the student body. This class has high withdrawal and failure rates. Sometimes it is called a "gatekeeper" class (Jenkins, Jaggars, and Roksa, 2009).

In this report the name used to describe classes that offer learning assistance activities specifically designed to support the students enrolled in them are called "target classes," as the learning assistance services are customized and "targeted" for serving students enrolled in that specific course. The focus is shifted from erroneously attempting to identify students at risk in the class to students in that particular class who are welcome to use the learning assistance activities to meet course expectations or as supplemental or enrichment experiences deepening their mastery of course content. Faculty members who teach this target class are involved to varying degrees with the learning assistance activities preparing students for academic success. (This aspect of faculty involvement is described later.)

## Prerequisite Acquisition of Knowledge and Skills

This first category of the three approaches operates as a prerequisite learning experience before the student enrolls in college-level courses such as college algebra, general psychology, or general biology. Activities include academic preparatory academies and remedial or developmental courses in English, reading,

**EXHIBIT 2**
**Categorizing Approaches of Learning Assistance**

| Institution Provides Prerequisite Acquisition of Knowledge and Skills Needed for College Success | Institution Provides Concurrent Acquisition of Knowledge and Skills Needed for College Success | Institution Provides Outsourcing to Acquire Knowledge and Skills Needed for College Success |
|---|---|---|
| Separate academic preparatory academy managed by the institution | Learning assistance offered as a **voluntary supplement** to the class targeted for academic support and center enrichment through a learning assistance or a peer cooperative learning program | Strengthened high school–college articulation agreements and higher exit skills from high school, thus reducing the need for college learning assistance |
| Remedial credit courses offered by a department in the institution | Learning assistance **closely coordinated** with the class targeted for academic support and enrichment through some learning communities such as linked classes and some peer cooperative learning programs | Some students seeking entry to four-year institutions self-select courses or are directed by the four-year institution to seek remedial or developmental skill development at local adult education centers or area two-year colleges |
| Developmental credit courses offered by a department in the institution | Learning assistance **embedded in** the course targeted for academic support and enrichment through some learning communities such as federated learning communities or faculty who infuse learning assistance in their core curriculum courses | Institution formally subcontracts learning assistance (tutoring, developmental-level courses) to another provider such as two-year colleges or commercial companies |

and mathematics. In the case of academic preparatory academies, participation precedes enrollment in any college-level courses or perhaps even admission to the postsecondary institution. Remedial and developmental courses may be taken while the student is simultaneously enrolled in other college-level courses. Successful completion of the remedial or developmental course, perhaps intermediate algebra, is often required by local college policy and serves as a prerequisite before enrollment in the college-level algebra course is permitted.

Just because a student scores low on a college entrance examination for one subject area does not mean that all his or her initial courses will be remedial or developmental. As described earlier, a student's academic skills lie along a continuum between novice and expert. Where the student is at the novice level, enrollment in a developmental course is essential, while in other academic areas they are average or perhaps expert.

**Academic Preparatory Academy.** Learning assistance is offered at a separate academic preparatory academy. Such academic preparatory academies first appeared in the early to mid-1800s, when four-year colleges often felt the need to provide the equivalent of a high school education for potential college students because public education was not widely available in the United States. Public two-year institutions were yet to become available for most people. Although these academies required enrollment by students for a year or more, some modern-day preparatory academies are shorter length. Academic bridge programs for high school seniors prepare them over the summer to be more successful during fall at college. Bridge programs are often hosted by four-year institutions (ERIC Clearinghouse on Higher Education, 2001). Research studies attest to the efficacy of such programs for improving students' academic success. Research studies have documented positive outcomes, including higher college grades and higher rates of graduation (Pascarella and Terenzini, 2005), stronger academic preparation and easier transition to college (Swail and Perna, 2002), and deeper connection with the college (McLure and Child, 1998).

Another factor favoring the effectiveness of these high school–college bridge programs is the seamless flow of the education experience for students. Analysis of the national grade-cohort longitudinal study by the National Center for Education Statistics found that college enrollment immediately following high school graduation increased college degree completion rates (Adelman, 2006). Maintaining academic focus by students continuing their education immediately increased the likelihood of their timely college graduation. A review of the professional literature revealed a successful case study of this approach by St. Thomas Aquinas College (Sparkill, New York), a four-year, independent institution. Academic Services (http://www.stac.edu/AcademicService.htm) provides traditional learning assistance services and hosts the summer academic preparatory academy. It focus on graduating high school seniors who share characteristics of TRIO students such as predominately first-generation college attendees, low family income, and other variables that place them at higher risk for attrition. Activities include developing academic skills and acculturating them to expectations for college. The summer period provides sufficient time to develop simultaneously their essential learning skills while enrolled in rigorous classes.

Modern incarnations of preparatory academies also include private commercial schools such as Kaplan and Sylvan Learning Systems. Public two-year colleges through their function of preparing students for successful transfer to senior institutions are another example.

**Remedial Courses.** These classes—basic reading, elements of English, and basic arithmetic—assume students possess fundamental cognitive deficits in need of remediation. These courses focus on academic content typically covered in middle school or early high school. At most institutions, these courses are a prerequisite before students may enroll in the next course in the academic sequence (Boylan, Bonham, and Bliss, 1994). Exit competencies of remedial courses generally prepare students for subsequent enrollment in a developmental course by teaching the needed skills and knowledge. For example, successful completion of a remedial course in fundamentals of mathematics provides a student with skills needed to enroll in an intermediate algebra course. Few students could complete the fundamentals of mathematics course and have a high chance of success in a college algebra course (Boylan, 2002b).

As described earlier in "History of Learning Assistance in U.S. Postsecondary Education," four-year institutions offered remedial courses during the 1800s to meet the needs of students with poor or nonexistent secondary education (Maxwell, 1979). These remedial courses moved to the two-year colleges when they spread across the United States during the early 1900s (Cohen and Brawer, 2002).

Few national research studies concern the effectiveness of remedial courses. A common finding among these studies is that these courses must be more integrated into the culture of the institution and bundled with other learning assistance activities. If they are not, outcomes are mixed for most students (Kulik, Kulik, and Schwalb, 1983; Roueche and Roueche, 1993, 1999). It is unreasonable to expect to overcome years of inadequate education or ineffective student effort in high school with a single remedial course. Without the provision of remedial and developmental courses, however, students from impoverished backgrounds and poorly funded rural and urban schools have less hope for success in college.

**Developmental Courses.** These courses, in contrast with remedial courses, focus on students' strengths, develop both cognitive and affective domains, and build skills necessary for success in college-level courses. Remedial courses look to the past and focus on acquiring the skills and knowledge that should have been obtained while in high school; developmental courses look to the future and the skills needed for success in college. Typical developmental courses include intermediate algebra, college textbook reading, learning strategies, and basic writing composition. These courses count toward meeting financial aid requirements and often receive institutional credit. About 10 percent of institutions allow them to fulfill graduation requirements (National Center for Education Statistics, 2003).

According to the National Center for Education Statistics (2003), two-year public institutions are the most common providers of developmental courses, with 98 percent offering them in one or more academic content areas. Eighty percent of public four-year institutions offer them. At private two-year institutions, the rate is 63 percent; it declines to 59 percent at four-year private institutions. The trend for these courses is relatively stable over the 1990s (National Center for Education Statistics, 1991, 1996, 2003), except for a steeper decline at public research universities (Barefoot, 2003).

Developmental courses are placed in the category of prerequisite acquisition approaches, because at most colleges students must successfully complete them before they are allowed to enroll in the next course in the academic sequence. For example, if the student scores low on college or institutional entrance exams in mathematics and is placed in intermediate algebra, he or she must successfully complete this course before being allowed to enroll in college algebra. Like for remedial courses, a student might be enrolled in a single developmental course during the academic term while all the other courses are college level, which is why students who are enrolled in these courses are not called "developmental students." Most students who enroll in these courses do so only in one academic content area (National Center for Education Statistics, 2003). Although they need development in one academic content area, they are college ready or advanced in other areas based on college or institutional entrance exams.

Sometimes students who enroll in these classes feel disconnected, perhaps because of the administrative location of the remedial or developmental course. No uniform pattern exists for location of these credit courses across the United States. At some institutions, the courses are taught in the academic departments of mathematics, psychology, or writing. At other institutions, the courses and other learning assistance activities are clustered in a separate academic or administrative unit in the institution (Boylan, Bonham, and Bliss, 1994).

A review of the professional literature identifies developmental courses as the most controversial and contested element of learning assistance. They have ignited fierce public debates between supporters and opponents. As described in one of the contemporary controversies, opponents of these courses question colleges dealing with learning competencies that should have been met while the student was in high school. With scarce funds for postsecondary education, spending money on instruction of remedial and developmental courses appears to duplicate efforts by the high school and waste precious resources. Another issue that critics raise with these courses is their effectiveness.

Although a review of the ERIC database and the professional literature reveals institutional studies affirming the efficacy of developmental courses, few national research studies are available of developmental courses. Older national studies found when developmental courses are offered separate from other learning assistance activities, the results are sometimes inconclusive (Kulik, Kulik, and Schwalb, 1983; Roueche and Roueche, 1993, 1999).

Bailey (2009) analyzed these courses with a national dataset and found them ineffective. Among his recommendations were more research on these courses and use of more noncredit learning assistance services such as peer study groups.

Several reasons are possible why analysis of developmental courses sometimes yields mixed or negative results. As stated earlier about remedial courses, it is unreasonable to expect that years of inadequate education or ineffective student effort in high school can be overcome by a single developmental course. A second reason may be a basic flaw in research design. Previous national studies (Bailey, 2009; Kulik, Kulik, and Schwalb, 1983; Roueche and Roueche, 1993, 1999) did not add variables to their analyses concerning attributes of the developmental courses and contexts in which they were offered. They did not have the ability to sort out poorly managed, average, or well-managed programs. When student data from all institutions are aggregated, it is not surprising to find inconclusive results. A finer level of analysis is needed for this complex issue. The only national study on developmental courses was sponsored through the Exxon Foundation in the late 1980s; it found these courses effective when they observed best practices and poor results for those that did not (Boylan, Bonham, and Bliss, 1994).

The bottom line is that more careful and detailed research is needed to understand developmental courses and the variables that affect their effectiveness. Proponents and opponents of developmental courses call for more research in this area (Bailey, 2009; Boylan, Saxon, Bonham, and Parks, 1993). As the most vexing and controversial element of learning assistance, this issue demands careful and detailed national study. It is one of the recommendations for action listed in the final chapter of this report.

A learning assistance approach that bridges the prerequisite acquisition approach of this section and the concurrent acquisition approach in the next is to place developmental courses in learning communities. To overcome disconnection that sometimes occurs for students in developmental courses with subsequent college-level courses in the academic sequence, some institutions place these courses in learning communities, integrating them with other college-level introductory courses (Malnarich and others, 2003). For example, a reading course might be paired with a reading-intensive course like introduction to psychology or world history. A rigorous study explored the impact of these learning communities. At Kingsborough Community College (part of the City University of New York), students scoring low on admission tests for English were placed in a learning community that included a developmental English course, a course in health or psychology, and a one-credit orientation course. Using a randomized trial that placed students in this learning community or a control group, the students in the experimental group experienced higher outcomes—enrolling in more courses, passing more classes, earning more college credits, and earning higher English test scores needed for a college degree (Scrivener and others, 2008).

### Concurrent Acquisition of Knowledge and Skills

The second learning assistance approach operates through concurrent learning experiences. Students simultaneously enroll in a college-level class, whether or not they have been identified as academically underprepared, and use learning assistance services to support their learning in that class. A common characteristic of such a class is academic rigor exceeding the average of other college-level classes. These courses are challenging for many students, and the classes have high withdrawal and failure rates. Sometimes they are called "gatekeeper" classes (Jenkins, Jaggars, and Roksa, 2009).

For purposes of this discussion, this historically difficult class is called a "target class," as learning assistance services are customized and "targeted" for serving students enrolled in that specific course. Other students in the same class that have not been identified as academically underprepared for content material in that particular class are welcome to use the learning assistance activities as supplemental or enrichment experiences to deepen mastery of course content. This concurrent acquisition approach is divided into three smaller groups of activities: those offered as supplemental learning experiences through the student's voluntary participation; those offered as a coordinated program that requires moderate involvement by the target course instructor; and those embedded, infused, or mainstreamed in the course targeted for academic support that thereby serve all students enrolled in the class, regardless of their academic preparation.

One of the activities described in the previous section on prerequisite acquisition approaches could also have appeared in this section. Because most students enroll in only a single developmental course, the rest of their courses are at the college level. These students concurrently develop competency through the developmental course while they advance their knowledge and skills through the college-level courses. The key issue that places developmental courses in the previous section is that students are not ready to enroll in the college-level course for which they are underprepared. They are, however, ready for enrollment in other college-level courses.

**Supplemental Learning Experiences.** These learning assistance services are self-selected by students who participate voluntarily. Three examples of this approach include learning assistance centers, peer cooperative learning groups, and tutoring. Learning assistance centers, especially those that coordinate and interact closely with course instructors, report positive results for students who participate (Boylan, 2002b; Continuous Quality Improvement Network/American Productivity and Quality Center, 2000; Maxwell, 1997; McCabe, 2000). These centers are one-stop locations for students to obtain tutoring, engage in self-paced instruction, use mediated instruction such as computer software to review basic course concepts, and engage in supplemental learning activities. Learning assistance centers often focus resources and personnel serving specific courses identified by faculty and student requests. These classes frequently have high rates of final course grades of D or F and course withdrawal. Limited institutional budgets often do not permit expansion of the learning assistance centers to the entire course curriculum. Learning assistance centers are used at Liberty University (Lynchburg, Virginia), a private, four-year institution. The Bruckner Learning Center (http://www.liberty.edu/academics/general/bruckner/) offers traditional learning assistance services. In addition, it has extensive holdings of audiovisual supplemental learning materials and self-paced learning modules promoted by faculty members for enrichment learning in targeted classes.

Use of campus learning centers to supplement learning in undergraduate education for those predicted to have academic difficulty is sometimes expanded to serve graduate students. This approach serves undergraduate, graduate, and professional school students, regardless of academic preparation. For example, the University of Pennsylvania (Philadelphia) is a private, four-year institution that offers advanced degrees, including Ph.D.s. Forty percent of the students served by the Weingarten Learning Resource Center (http://www.vpul.upenn.edu/lrc) are graduate and professional students in dentistry, medicine, and veterinary science. A two-week writing retreat called "dissertation boot camp" brings together dissertation writers from across the twelve graduate schools and provides them with mentors, project planning, and writing support. The transitions workshop for the Medical School attracts nearly every professional school student in dentistry, medicine, and veterinary science to develop learning strategies essential for success in the academically rigorous programs. Learning assistance centers appear at both four-year and two-year institutions (Christ, 1971, 1997). Such centers, along with tutoring programs, may be the primary provider of learning assistance at four-year institutions that choose not to offer developmental courses.

Another expression of supplemental learning is provided through peer cooperative learning groups. One type of peer group depends on voluntary student participation. The study group is offered in an academically rigorous class with high rates of final course grades of D or F and course withdrawals. Numerous studies attest to their efficacy and note their use at two-year and four-year institutions (Arendale, 2005a). One widely implemented example of this approach is supplemental instruction (http://www.umke.edu/cad/si). Supplemental instruction is used at more than 2,500 postsecondary institutions in forty-five countries to provide a study review session that integrates review of rigorous course material with modeling of appropriate learning strategies for students' adoption and independent use. Another similar approach is structured learning assistance (http://www.ferris.edu/sla/home page.htm). It shares common features with supplemental instruction, except that it requires attendance in the weekly study review group by all students enrolled in the target class until the first major examination. Afterward, attendance is voluntary except for those with a failing course grade.

The third example of voluntary learning assistance is individual or group tutoring. It is the oldest of all learning assistance approaches and nearly universal at every postsecondary institution (Gordon and Gordon, 1990). Tutoring programs were reported at three-quarters of all institutions, with a slightly higher rate at four-year schools (74.1 percent) than two-year schools (71.1 percent) (Boylan, Bonham, and Bliss, 1992). In a national study, tutoring was found to significantly improve persistence and graduation rates, final course grades in the course tutored, higher completion rates in the course tutored, and higher interest by students in the academic content matter where they were tutored (Boylan, Bonham, and Bliss, 1992).

All three of these activities depend on higher motivation by participants because of the reliance on voluntary self-selection; a major disadvantage is that students who do not generally seek help do not participate. They are then at higher risk for academic failure (Dembo and Seli, 2004). Sometimes the students who most need to participate do not do so. For example, although supplemental instruction attracts nearly equal percentages of students from the lower, middle, and upper ranges of composite ACT scores, only about a third of each category participate at least once during the academic term. For students from the bottom one-third of the ACT composite score, two-thirds of these students do not attend a single time (Martin and Arendale, 1997). Students who do attend regularly throughout the semester benefit in comparison with those who never or seldom attend (Congos and Schoeps, 1998). It is not surprising that more time on task results in higher student outcomes. Increasing the structure of the activity is the reason that structured learning assistance requires mandatory attendance for students initially in the course; some colleges modify their supplemental instruction programs to do the same (Hodges, Dochen, and Donna, (2001). More work is required to modify voluntary learning assistance activities to more effectively attract and serve more students.

**Coordinated Program with the Target Class.**  Rather than relying on voluntary participation, this second cluster of learning activities requires participation by all students enrolled in the class because of its academic rigor and historic rates of academic difficulty by a wide range of students. These learning activities often occur outside the target class session but are closely coordinated with the course instructor.

In one variation of a coordinated learning assistance program, a "learning community" is formed by linking a course focusing on learning strategies with a college-level course such as general psychology. Doing so requires concurrent enrollment of students in both courses (Malnarich and others, 2003; Tinto, 1998). The textbook readings and work requirements from a psychology course provide context for applying cognitive learning strategies acquired from the linked study strategies course, providing immediate application of the learning strategies in a real-world and academically rigorous course. Studies demonstrate efficacy of this approach, and it has been identified as a best practice (Continuous Quality Improvement Network/American Productivity and Quality Center, 2000; McCabe and Day, 1998; Tinto, 1998). One four-year institution successfully using this approach is Indiana University of Pennsylvania. Learning assistance services of the Department of Developmental Studies (http://www.iup.edu/devstudies/) include traditional learning assistance activities and linked courses. A core curriculum course is linked with an applied learning strategies course.

A second variation of the coordinated learning assistance program requires students' participation in additional discussion sessions attached to historically difficult courses with high rates of academic failure as measured by final course grades. This approach includes several common features:

All students in the class are required to participate.

Study sessions are closely supervised.

Curriculum is coordinated by a faculty member.

Sessions are led by a trained peer student

Sessions integrate both academic content and learning strategy practice. This approach improves on voluntary supplemental learning activities described previously by ensuring that all students in the target class participate, especially those least likely to elect the opportunity. Two national models illustrating this approach are the emerging scholars program (Treisman, 1986) and peer-led team learning (http://pltl.org). The former was initially developed at the University of California, Berkeley to serve students of color in academically rigorous math, science, and engineering majors. Since then, the program has expanded to many campuses by serving all students enrolling in targeted classes and academic programs. Peer-led team learning serves all students in rigorous introductory science courses such as in chemistry. Hundreds of colleges across the United States employ these postsecondary peer cooperative learning programs. Rigorous research studies have reported improved student outcomes as a result (Arendale, 2005a).

Peer-led team learning was developed at the City University of New York in 1993. Support through a grant from the National Science Foundation assisted more than one hundred institutions in implementing it. The design of the method increases students' academic success, specifically with introductory chemistry courses. These courses often serve as gatekeepers for rigorous science degrees. Student-leaders (peers) guide the activities of small groups of students during weekly workshops. Students work challenging problems through cooperative learning activities. Peer leaders are trained to engage students actively and productively with the material and with each other. This methodology offers a number of educational opportunities. The format encourages questions and discussions leading to deeper conceptual understanding. Students learn to work in teams and communicate more effectively. And peer leaders learn teaching and group management skills (Arendale, 2005a).

**Embedded in the Target Course.** In this set of activities, the course instructor directly integrates learning assistance in the classroom experience for all students. Rather than requiring students to complete prerequisite courses or engage in additional out-of-class activities as described in other models, course instructors integrate activities in their courses in history, science, literature, and the like. Two expressions of this model are federated learning communities (Malnarich and others, 2003) and the University of Minnesota General College (Higbee, Lundell, and Arendale, 2005). The course curriculum and the classroom environment are transformed through simultaneous instruction in academic content and learning strategies. This seamless integration provides an enriched learning experience for all students in the course without the need for prerequisite or adjunct learning experiences for students and the institution, thereby saving time and expense.

An example from this approach is the introductory U.S. and world history courses taught at the University of Minnesota. A small sample of activities from the classes include providing complete copies of PowerPoint lecture slides and recording class sessions and posting both to the course Web site. Students are able to focus more on class discussion and take notes on that conversation than on copying each PowerPoint slide. Students can replay lectures if they miss a class or relisten to them. Providing the PowerPoint slides and recording the class lectures was initially provided to meet requests of new immigrant students and some students with vision challenges. Availability was expanded to all students in the class and is used widely. Other examples of integrating learning assistance support include students' working in teams to create a weekly audio podcast and an exam preparation Web site to review course content before exams. Instructors integrate use of graphic organizers, model different styles of taking lecture notes, and debrief mock examinations to develop test-taking skills (Arendale and Ghere, 2008).

### Outsourced Learning Assistance

In this final category, campus policymakers eliminate the need for the institution to offer credit courses in remedial or developmental skills. This approach has three expressions: strengthening high school–college articulation, encouraging students to seek assistance elsewhere, and subcontracting remedial or developmental courses to commercial companies or nearby community colleges.

**Strengthening High School–College Articulation.** In this approach, institutional leaders and state policymakers shift responsibility for traditional developmental courses to secondary education. Achieve (http://www.achieve.org) is a major national organization that was created in the mid-1990s by business leaders and state governors to foster these objectives.

The approach has several common activities (Achieve, 2007a):

Appoint articulation and transfer task forces to examine standards for high school graduation.

Administer high-stakes high school exit tests to validate academic rigor of the high school graduation certificate.

Organize professional development programs for high school teachers to effectively implement best practices of learning assistance and basic academic skill development in their courses.

Initiate ongoing conversations between high school teachers and their counterparts in college teaching similar courses to eliminate gaps between skill mastery upon exit from high school and entrance expectations at college.

Annual surveys of all states find considerable progress in reaching these objectives (Achieve, 2007b). Often these practices encourage more academically rigorous high school courses that correlate with higher college graduation rates (Adelman, 2006). Considerable energy has been devoted to increasing conversation among all stakeholders on the educational pathway. Many states have P–16 commissions that improve transitions from preschool through graduation from college.

**Learning Assistance at Other Venues.** A passive approach to outsourcing is directing students to select another education provider or institution to obtain needed learning assistance: for example, local adult education centers offering adult basic education and GED instruction and credit and noncredit programming at local public community colleges. Outsourcing learning assistance to local community colleges is somewhat successful. Students are sometimes able to travel to the nearby community college to complete the developmental course and then transfer the course credit to the senior institution. At some four-year institutions, the local community college offers developmental courses on the four-year institution's campus. In other cases, students complete a significant amount of coursework or earn a transfer degree at the community college. It is important to note, however, that "swirling" or nomadic attendance at multiple institutions is a significant negative factor for degree completion, according to the most recent national grade-cohort longitudinal study by the National Center for Education Statistics (Adelman, 2006).

Florida has the oldest and best-evaluated program of outsourcing all developmental courses from four-year public institutions to the state community college system (Furlong and Fleishman, 2000). Except for Florida A&M—which retains authority to offer such courses—developmental courses are offered by the community college on the university campus. A careful evaluation of the collaborative program identified key features that support success (Furlong and Fleishman, 2000):

Sound administration of the college-university agreements.

Clear communication between the two-year and four-institution.

Effective delivery of services to students.

Community colleges that are perceived best suited for delivery of remedial instruction.

A majority of students successfully performing college-level coursework after completing college preparatory courses.

**Outsourced to a Commercial Company.** An early experiment with outsourcing developmental courses occurred in the late 1980s through the 1990s by commercial companies. As described earlier, a small number of proprietary, two-year, and four-year institutions contracted with Kaplan and Sylvan Learning Systems in the mid-1990s to provide instruction in developmental mathematics, reading, and writing (Blumenstyk, 2006; Gose, 1997; Maryland Higher Education Commission, 1997). The pilot programs ended because costs greatly exceeded salaries of adjunct college instructors who could be assigned large classes (Blumenstyk, 2006; Boylan, 2002a).

Another round of outsourcing learning assistance–related services is occurring today. The focus has moved from outsourcing developmental courses to outsourcing tutoring. Meeting outcomes of the No Child Left Behind federal requirements led some public school districts to outsource their tutorial services to local commercial vendors (Segal, 2004). Following this example, some colleges are contracting tutorial and writing assistance services to commercial companies such as SmartThinking (http://www.smarthinking.com/). This commercial service purports to serve on-campus students as well as distance learners.

During this experiment with outsourcing, commercial companies learned from strategic errors made in offering college courses during the first wave in the mid-1990s. Commercial companies avoid the expensive option of offering developmental credit courses or academic tutors onsite at the local institution. Instead, they offer online tutoring. This simpler approach has several advantages:

It avoids investment in creating course curriculum customized for each institution.

It avoids hiring expensive on-site tutors or instructors who serve only students at the individual site.

The company can more efficiently hire tutors and other helpers to serve student users at a variety of locations through the United States.

Often the commercial company's contract fee is based on the potential number of users of the service at the entire institution rather than the number who actually use it.

Some state college systems contract for online tutorial services. One example is Minnesota State Colleges and Universities, which represents all public state community and four-year institutions except the University of Minnesota System. It represents more than forty institutions and has contracted with SmartThinking to provide a fixed number of monthly hours of online tutorial services to member schools that underwrite part of the contract cost. A limited number of tutorial hours are allocated monthly to each participating institution. Each institution sets its own rules concerning how many hours each student at the school may use to access the service during a month. This system supports both on-campus and distance learning students.

Some learning assistance professionals are concerned that commercial online tutoring might justify replacing traditional onsite tutoring that employs full-time professional tutors and part-time paraprofessional student tutors. No evidence suggests that it has occurred, however. Many students served through online tutoring are distance learners or working adults unable to access campus onsite tutoring. Minnesota State Colleges and Universities plans to offer 25 percent of its courses online by 2020. Providing student services for distance learners such as online tutoring is essential. Some empirical studies support the efficacy of online tutoring (Roberts, 2009).

Online tutoring programs encounter the same challenges as voluntary on-campus tutoring programs. Students who may most need the service may not use it because they lack the motivation to seek help. Additionally, online tutoring requires the use of technology, which not everyone is comfortable with. Studies of online tutoring identified challenges with the pedagogy resulting from low rates of use (Williams, 2005), loss of social presence with asynchronous tutoring (Mercer, 2002), inattention to tutees' learning needs (Sawaan, 2006), and other difficulties (Sandvik, 2007). Rather than dismissing it because of its initial challenges, experiments with online learning assistance services such as tutoring and online developmental courses need to accelerate. They warrant careful research, scrutiny by peer-reviewed publications, and careful monitoring of the impact of such systems and best practices to guide them.

# The Institution's Requirements for Change

The varied approaches of learning assistance require different levels of institutional resources, including the amount of change asked of the faculty member who teaches a class targeted for additional academic support and enrichment. As a natural consequence of these approaches, differing levels of improved student outcomes emerge such as higher academic achievement, persistence in an academic degree program, and timely completion of the academic degree. Institutional resources are critical for increasing the success of learning assistance by improving student outcomes. As described in the following chapter, the institution must provide the needed resources for successful learning assistance programs.

Exhibit 3 compares six levels of integration of learning assistance in a class targeted for academic support and enrichment. It draws on earlier work by Keimig (1983), Boylan (2002b), and others creating similar learning assistance models.

The first column identifies the six levels of integration of learning assistance in the class targeted for academic support. Moving from the bottom to the top, each level requires higher levels of activity and involvement by faculty and administration. Levels One and Two do not involve faculty members, as the activities occur outside the classroom. Campus learning assistance staff or faculty members managing the services coordinate the activities. Typical activities include voluntary remedial classes, tutoring, and study skill workshops. In Level Three, the faculty member teaching the target class needing learning assistance and the counterpart instructing the prerequisite developmental course coordinate their curriculum. They coordinate exit competencies in the developmental class to meet entrance knowledge and skill expectations of the entry-level core curriculum target class. Most change occurs for the faculty member teaching the developmental course regarding curriculum and pedagogy. Accurate placement in developmental courses requires accurate college

**EXHIBIT 3**
**Hierarchy of Learning Assistance Approaches**

| Increasing Levels of Integration in the Target Course | Increasing Intensity Levels of Learning Assistance Approaches | Involvement by Target Class Faculty Member | Likelihood of Improved Student Outcomes |
|---|---|---|---|
| Level Six: Transformed target class environment through an embedded and comprehensive learning assistance system | Seamless integration of learning assistance in the class by approaches such as Universal Instructional Design and the General College model. Traditional learning centers expand their mission by supporting faculty to provide their own learning assistance in the target class. | Heavy and sustained | High |
| Level Five: Mandatory supplemental activities for the target class | Heavily coordinated learning assistance program attached to the target class through mandatory attendance of students in programs like ESP and PLTL | Significant | ↑ |
| Level Four: Voluntary supplemental activities for the target class | Lightly coordinated learning assistance program attached to the target class through voluntary attendance of students in programs such as supplemental instruction | Limited | ↑ |

(Continued)

**EXHIBIT 3 (Continued)**

| Increasing Levels of Integration in the Target Course | Increasing Intensity Levels of Learning Assistance Approaches | Involvement by Target Class Faculty Member | Likelihood of Improved Student Outcomes |
|---|---|---|---|
| Level Three: Prerequisite developmental class preparing students for the target class | Developmental class in an area such as English, science, or mathematics, with the curriculum coordinated by the faculty who teach the target and developmental class | Limited | ↑ |
| Level Two: Learning assistance for individual students outside the target class | Drop-in tutoring that occurs outside the target class | None | ↑ |
| Level One: Isolated development of remedial skills | Services offered to the general student body such as study skill classes or workshops, reading classes, and remedial classes | None | Low |

admission assessment testing. Additional assessment at the end of the term ensures mastery of needed skills before enrolling in subsequent courses in academic sequence. For example, before students successfully exit the developmental math class, they must demonstrate mastery of skills needed for success in a college algebra class. In addition, the faculty member of the subsequent college-level course may administer a customized assessment on the first day of class to ensure proper placement of students.

Levels Four and Five connect supplemental learning assistance activities with target classes that are part of the core curriculum with high rates of final course grades of D or F and withdrawal. Activities involve coordination and revision of the curriculum. Level Four activities dominated the field of learning assistance in the 1970s and 1980s with few exceptions. Students eagerly and voluntarily participated as they were able to identify their academic weaknesses. In the 1990s, Level Five activities increased mandatory involvement by all students in the target classes. The basis for these activities rests on decades of research indicating students most needing learning assistance are least likely to seek it. It is common for less than a third of students identified as least academically prepared to participate voluntarily in supplemental non-credit learning assistance (Arendale, 2005a).

Level Six transforms the classroom learning environment through an embedded and comprehensive learning assistance system. In the previous five levels of class integration, varying levels of change are required by the faculty member for the target class. At this highest level, this faculty member assumes primary responsibility for creating a learning environment conducive for mastery learning by students of a wide range of academic preparation levels. Universal Instructional Design (UID) is one model that mainstreams students with disabilities into traditional classrooms. The learning assistance community significantly adapts and broadens UID to serve all students in a course. Silver, Bourke, and Strehorn (1998) illustrate how UID expands learning modalities and creates an enriched learning environment for those with disabilities as well as all other students. Scott, McGuire, and Shaw (2003) identify nine UID principles. Based on emerging UID literature and research, Higbee (2003) and others apply UID as progressive learning assistance for all students. Learning assistance activities are integrated in the course curriculum through the classroom faculty member.

The third column in Exhibit 3 identifies the level of involvement by those teaching the target class. Historically the approach in Levels One through Four has dominated learning assistance. In the past decade, increases have occurred in Levels Five and Six learning assistance approaches. Increasingly in areas of science, technology, engineering, and mathematics, faculty members directly involve themselves with coordinating and providing academic support for their students fueled by recognition that past approaches are ineffective in supporting academic achievement and persistence of their students in rigorous academic programs, especially for historically underrepresented student populations.

The final column in Exhibit 3 predicts the likelihood of improved student outcomes such as academic achievement, persistence in an academic major, and graduation with a degree. Many evaluation studies document that increasing the integration of learning assistance in the target class results in higher student outcomes (Boylan 1999, 2002b; Continuous Quality Improvement Network/American Productivity and Quality Center, 2000; Farmer and Barham, 2001; Keimig, 1983; Koski and Levin, 1998; McCabe, 2003). These higher levels of success require more faculty involvement and institutional resources to achieve desired outcomes. Some evaluation studies find inconclusive results for remedial courses in Level Two and developmental courses in Level Three.

The hierarchy shown in Exhibit 3 roughly mirrors the history of learning assistance in U.S. postsecondary education. The first learning assistance activities were individual and group tutoring followed by study skill workshops. They form the first two levels of the hierarchy. When learning assistance was introduced in U.S. postsecondary education, it did not involve core curriculum faculty members. In the 1800s remedial courses were introduced in four-year institutions, and developmental credit courses were added to the college curriculum. These courses began to shift out of four-year institutions and were offered in nearly all two-year colleges—the third level of the hierarchy. With the explosive growth of college enrollment after World War II, learning assistance expanded with voluntary and mandatory participation activities that were attached to historically difficult courses. They form Levels Four and Five of the hierarchy. The final level of the hierarchy requires faculty members to be active in the process and to be agents for embedding learning assistance activities in their classrooms. Some reports are available of faculty members' involvement in Level Six learning assistance activities employing UID to meet the needs of students with different levels of academic preparation and students with disabilities (Higbee, 2003; Higbee and Goff, 2008).

## Summary

One of the great advantages of the U.S. postsecondary education system is wide autonomy in its mission. It is also one of its weaknesses. Tremendous variety exists among institutions regarding provision of learning assistance— prerequisite, concurrent, outsourced, or a combination of these approaches. This chapter has identified a wide range of these approaches. Although availability is nearly universal at every institution, categories and level of intensity differ widely. Stratifying learning assistance in higher education contributes to stratifying opportunity for students and uneven rates of student achievement and graduation. A key factor for higher student outcomes is higher involvement by faculty members teaching core curriculum courses. The following chapter identifies current best practices in learning assistance as well as the investment in time, personnel, and resources the institution needs to achieve desired institutional and student outcomes.

# Best Practices and Models
# in Learning Assistance

A WIDE VARIETY OF LEARNING ASSISTANCE flourishes in U.S. postsecondary institutions. The previous chapter categorized individual activities into three approaches for meeting students' needs. Although a review of the ERIC database identifies thousands of learning assistance reports, it is confusing and inefficient to scan through individual institutional reports to discover specific practices. Evidence-based practices based on successful use at multiple institutions are needed in addition to the identification of best practices. This chapter identifies traditional and emerging educational theories guiding such practices. Effective theory and pedagogy are the foundations for best practices.

One method to deal with the increasing volume of data about learning assistance can be found in the business world. For businesspeople, best practices are policies, principles, standards, and procedures leading companies use to perform at the highest level. Leading companies are designated as those operating among the top 10 percent of their comparable peers. During the 1950s and 1960s, business experts in the United States and Japan focused on quality and continuous improvement. Companies emulated the actions of top companies. The Japanese word is *kaizan*, the philosophy of continuous and never-ending improvement.

Commonly accepted principles for improved learning of college students serve as guides for identifying best practices. Chickering and Gamson (1987) identified seven principles for good practice in undergraduate education:

Encourage frequent contact between students and faculty in and out of class.

Facilitate cooperation among students because learning is a social process.

Promote active learning through social interaction and engagement with the content material.

Give prompt feedback to students to allow them to reflect and make changes in behavior.

Increase time on task to increase higher outcomes.

Communicate high expectations to prompt extra effort by learners.

Respect diverse talents and ways of learning.

Blimling and Whitt (1999) extended several of these best practices outside the classroom by identifying seven principles of good practice in student affairs:

Engage in active learning.

Develop coherent values and ethical standards.

Set and communicate high learning expectations.

Use systematic inquiry to improve performance.

Use resources effectively to achieve institutional mission and goals.

Forge educational partnerships among stakeholders.

Build supportive and inclusive communities.

This chapter sorts the professional literature concerning best practices of learning assistance into several sections. Emerging educational theories and pedagogies promoting positive student outcomes serve as foundation for and guide to individual best practices that follow.

## Educational Theories and Pedagogies

Appropriate and effective educational theory leads exemplary best practices to achieve the most positive outcomes for both the institution and the student (Hamrick, Evans, and Schuh, 2002). Fresh approaches reflect rapidly changing needs of a diverse student population. Following is a sample of emerging educational theories guiding best practices in learning assistance approaches and programs (Higbee, Arendale, and Lundell, 2005). Some theories focus on changing students' behaviors; others demand changes by the institution regarding curriculum delivery and the learning environment (Higbee, Arendale, and Lundell, 2005; Lundell and Higbee, 2001).

## Theories That Guide Students' Behaviors

The concept of "situated cognition" recognizes that students learn most effectively when they are in a learning environment perceived as personally meaningful and structured so they can directly apply new cognitive skills and strategies (Wilson, 1993). Students acquire and incorporate learning and study strategies more effectively when they concurrently apply them in the context of rigorous core curriculum courses (Stahl, Simpson, and Hayes, 1992). This approach differs significantly from prerequisite models of learning assistance such as remedial courses, study skill workshops, and the like. Disconnected prerequisite approaches erect barriers for students to acquire strategies and improve academic performance. Many do not link the immediate application of these new skills with demands presented in core curriculum courses. Situated cognition immediately grounds new abstract ideas and skills in concrete use with a learning task and an educational outcome measure. Immediate application and positive feedback heighten likelihood of further use.

Differing from previous models of learning assistance, new educational theories guide students as they actively manage their learning experiences. Metacognitive processes empower students to self-monitor comprehension of the material and equip them to select appropriate learning strategies based on demands of the academic task (Weinstein, Goetz, and Alexander, 1988). Metacognitive approaches address different types of motivation influencing students (Pintrich, 2000). This theory partially explains the effectiveness of peer cooperative learning programs like the emerging scholars program and supplemental instruction that blend active engagement, self-reflection about learning, and acquisition of new cognitive learning skills.

## Theories That Guide Instructors' Behaviors

Decisions made by classroom instructors significantly affect the learning environment. Unlike previous models of assistance that separated students into prerequisite learning venues, progressive approaches embrace an inclusive classroom. Universal Instructional Design (Higbee, 2003) has emerged as a guiding theory for transforming the classroom for a diverse student body. UID was originally designed to mainstream students with disabilities into traditional classrooms by reducing barriers (Silver, Bourke, and Strehorn, 1998). As illustrated in the previous chapter by the introductory history courses at the University of Minnesota, UID guides integration of learning assistance activities and mastery of metacognitive learning strategies for all students enrolled in target core curriculum classes. This strategy builds on effective learning theory requiring immediate application to promote internalization and continued use by the student.

Astin (1984, 1985) promotes the "talent development" theory of student development. Too often students are stereotyped, especially those needing learning assistance, as being deficient. The purpose of education is to add what they lack. Instead, Astin encourages educators to understand students' strengths and build on them rather than dwelling on what they temporarily lack. This shift from a deficit to a talent development model lifts stigma placed on students using learning assistance activities.

UID serves students identified as academically underprepared in one or more traditional core-curriculum classes. UID classes present rigorous academic content and require sophisticated skills (Higbee, 2003; Higbee, Lundell, and Arendale, 2005). Academically underprepared students can thrive through an enriched learning experience and embedded instruction of learning strategies. Rather than focusing on individual students and their perceived deficits, this educational model redirects the institution to improve the learning environment for all students. This systems approach avoids negative stigma previous learning assistance approaches often endured—a stigma that also generated negative consequences for the programs and the struggling students.

Another important educational theory enhancing learning is multiculturalism. The classroom learning environment shifts from one that reflects the dominant campus culture to one focused on individual students. Previously multiculturalism celebrated contributions by individuals from historically underrepresented groups in society through history appreciation months or assigned readings. Leading-edge theorists advocate radical redesign of the classroom learning experience for all students. As UID reduces barriers for all students through careful redesign of class learning tasks and activities, multiculturalism requires similar effort (Higbee and Goff, 2008). Just as physical barriers in the classroom present challenges for some students, so too do learning pedagogies that do not respect different cultures and preferred ways of interacting in a classroom setting. The urgency of this theory's application to learning assistance lies in the idea that it is a more effective way to serve a diverse student body. Culture extends beyond ethnicity through the expression of the multiple identities each person possesses. Some ways to implement instructional change guided by this theory include ensuring curricular materials reflect the diversity of the ethnicities, cultures, genders, and other identities of the students enrolled as well as the broader society; employing a variety of assessment activities such as objective exams, writing expressions, oral presentations, and the creation of Web sites to create opportunities for students to demonstrate mastery of course skills and knowledge; and providing various modes of learner interactions such as class lectures, large-group discussions, small-group discussions, and Internet-based conversations. Multiculturalism reflects a respect for a wide variety of ways to learn, express, and demonstrate mastery of rigorous course material sensitive to preferences from students' cultural backgrounds (Higbee, Lundell, and Duranczyk, 2003).

## Evidence-Based Best Practices

Effective learning theories guide best practices to improve achievement. This section identifies those practices consistent with the theories described earlier. During the 1980s, two major studies established the first best practices based on data from multiple institutions. The first published study was by the Noel-Levitz Center (Noel, Levitz, and Kaufmann, 1982). Data were gathered through an analysis of institutional data and consultations with college administrators regarding best practices for student recruitment and retention. Some were directly applicable to learning assistance. In 1984 the University of Texas conducted a national survey to identify common factors promoting success for students identified as academically underprepared (Roueche, Baker, and Roueche, 1984).

During the 1990s, these previous studies were confirmed and expanded. Several national studies focused attention on concurrent development of academic skills for students while enrolled in rigorous core curriculum courses (Boylan,

1999; Koski and Levin, 1998, Malnarich and others, 2003). Arendale (2001) conducted a national research study of more than four hundred two-year and four-year colleges that implemented supplemental instruction. McCabe (2000) conducted a study of twenty-five community colleges located throughout the United States regarding best practices for learning assistance. For the past two decades, the Council for the Advancement of Standards in Higher Education (Miller, 1999; Council for the Advancement of Standards, 2009) and the National Association for Developmental Education (Clark-Thayer and Cole, 2009) have developed national standards for best practices in learning assistance. The methodology for both organizations includes field studies and expert panel interviews to identify best practices for the field. The organizations repeated the process to verify and expand best practices and measures to evaluate their outcomes with students.

The most extensive national research study concerning best practices in learning assistance (Boylan, Bonham, and Bliss, 1992) was issued by the National Center for Developmental Education (NCDE, Boone, North Carolina) and funded by the Exxon Education Foundation. The study involved a carefully selected stratified sample group of 150 institutions of various types. Detailed information was collected on students entering college during fall 1984; the study followed them through spring 1990. Outcome variables included college grade point averages, pass rates of students enrolled in the first college-level courses in the same subject as the developmental course, and graduation rates. The American Continuous Quality Improvement Network (ACQIN) completed another national study in 2000. This association, comprising leading higher education institutions, contracted with the nonprofit American Productivity and Quality Center (APQC, Houston, Texas) to conduct the study. The APQC identified exemplar institutions and conducted detailed analyses to identify best practices. Dr. Hunter Boylan of the NCDE served as subject matter expert. Findings from these and other studies involving the NCDE were synthesized to present best practices for the field (Boylan, 2002b; Continuous Quality Improvement Network/American Productivity and Quality Center, 2000).

Several national projects and leaders in the field conducted multiinstitutional studies and issued findings that also identified exemplary institutions

(Casazza and Silverman, 1996; Farmer and Barham, 2001; Higbee, 2003; Higbee, Lundell, and Duranczyk, 2003; McCabe, 2003; McCabe and Day, 1998; Muraskin, 1997).

## Categories of Best Practices

National studies have identified approximately fifty best learning assistance practices. These individual best practices are categorized into six groups: organizational and administrative decisions; essential program components; critical instructional practices; important personnel practices; rigorous evaluation procedures; and necessary institutional practices, policies, and culture. The learning assistance staff or classroom instructors implement some best practices. Some are the responsibility of the learning assistance center or departmental administrator. Others involve upper-level campus administrators. Adopting other strategies as well enhances the impact of some practices. Adopting multiple best practices raises the likelihood of students' increased academic achievement and higher revenue generation by the institution through fees paid by students as they persist toward graduation.

Implementing best practices can improve the campus learning climate, and learning assistance is most effective when perceived as a campuswide responsibility. Embracing this perspective is Kirkwood Community College (Cedar Rapids, Iowa), a two-year public institution with approximately 12,000 students.

**EXHIBIT 4**
**Categories of Best Practices in Learning Assistance**

| Category of Best Practice | Responsibility Level within the Institution |
|---|---|
| Organizational and administrative best practices | Departmental and upper |
| Essential program components | Departmental |
| Critical instructional practices | Classroom |
| Important personnel practices | Departmental and upper |
| Rigorous evaluation procedures | Departmental |
| Necessary institutional practices, policies, and culture | Upper |

Learning Services (http://www.kirkwood.edu/) reports to Academic Affairs. Learning Services (LS) is an academic unit led by a dean reporting directly to the vice president of instruction. Appointing a high-ranking administer for the LS program both raises its profile and provides more integration and collaboration with other campuswide academic programs. Campuswide policies essential for LS include mandatory academic assessment of all entering students, course placement policies based on their assessments, and academic support for both traditional academic areas such as math and writing and technical programs in health and culinary arts. Other campuswide services include tutoring, supplemental instruction, disability services, and TRIO-funded student support services. Some key factors support the LS program's effectiveness: administrative placement of LS with academic affairs provides more resources for the unit, and high-level administrative support of LS places it on equal footing with other academic units reporting directly to the vice president. The campus learning environment is deeply influenced by the work of LS.

### Organizational and Administrative Best Practices

Several organizational and administrative best practices have been identified:

Central administration and organization of learning assistance activities and program (Arendale, 2001; Boylan, 2002b);

Consolidation of developmental courses, tutoring, and learning center activities (Boylan, 2002b; McCabe and Day, 1998);

Appointment of a campuswide learning assistance administrator (Boylan, 2002b);

Learning assistance guided by a mission, goals, and strategic plan (Boylan, 2002b; Clark-Thayer and Cole, 2009; Miller, 1999);

Establishment of a campuswide advisory board to provide feedback to improve services (Clark-Thayer and Cole, 2009; Miller, 1999);

Collaboration and coordination with other campus groups sharing similar goals such as a first-year experiences program, enrollment management, academic advising, counseling services, admissions office, and new-student orientation (Boylan, 2002b; Clark-Thayer and Cole, 2009; McCabe, 2000; McCabe and Day, 1998; Miller, 1999).

A theme of these practices involves careful coordination and consolidation. Although many colleges offer various forms of learning assistance activities, a smaller number centralize these activities. Too often, consolidated programs operate independently on campus and fail to collaborate with other units with similar goals and resources that could be leveraged to increase service to students. Consolidation offers efficiencies and reduces duplication of services. Collaboration with other units is also critical. Collaborating helps learning assistance programs that have sometimes operated at the margins of the college to become more nested in the campus learning environment. In addition, collaboration creates powerful allies for support, resources, and team building to increase desired student outcomes. An example of collaboration occurs at Adams State College (Alamosa, Colorado). Learning assistance activities are placed in the First Year Experience and Engagement Program (http://www.adams.edu/students/fyee/). This organizational decision places all programs serving first-year students in an integrated program. The synergy created through this model promotes higher use of learning assistance and reduces possible stigma for its use because of its association with the other first-year experience programs that serve all entering students.

In addition to investing in personnel and resources for direct provision of service, an essential requirement for this clustering of practices is assigning a high-ranking administrative placement for the program. A learning assistance program administrator appointed at the dean or executive cabinet level provides visibility, resources, and political influence. This administrative commitment may be more challenging than just creating higher numbers of direct service providers to students. Because of budget constraints and attempts to flatten the administrative structure of many institutions, adding additional high-ranking administrators is difficult, but the challenges and complexities of comprehensive learning assistance programs encourage this commitment.

### Essential Program Components

After establishing essential organizational and administrative structures that are the foundation of an effective learning assistance programs, attention should be placed on essential program components:

Developmental credit courses (Boylan, 2002b; Clark-Thayer and Cole, 2009; Farmer and Barham, 2001; Roueche, Baker, and Roueche, 1984);

Articulation between exit competencies in developmental courses and corresponding first-year college-level courses (Boylan, 2002b; Clark-Thayer and Cole, 2009; Farmer and Barham, 2001; McCabe, 2000; Miller, 1999; Roueche, Baker, and Roueche, 1984);

Drop-in learning assistance centers (Boylan, 2002b);

Group and individual tutoring (Arendale, 2001; Boylan, 2002b; Clark-Thayer and Cole, 2009; Roueche, Baker, and Roueche, 1984);

An academic alert program monitoring students' academic progress and initiating quick interventions (Boylan, 2002b; Farmer and Barham, 2001; Roueche, Baker, and Roueche, 1984);

Supplemental programs attached to historically difficult courses (Arendale, 2001; Boylan, 2002b; Clark-Thayer and Cole, 2009);

Students' mandatory attendance in supplemental learning activities predicted for academic risk (Arendale, 2001; Clark-Thayer and Cole, 2009);

Mandatory assessment of affective and cognitive skills for all students (Boylan, 2002b; Clark-Thayer and Cole, 2009; Farmer and Barham, 2001; McCabe, 2000; Miller, 1999; Noel, Levitz, and Kaufmann, 1982);

Mandatory placement in developmental courses of students identified through student assessment (Boylan, 2002b; Clark-Thayer and Cole, 2009; Farmer and Barham, 2001; McCabe, 2000; Roueche, Baker, and Roueche, 1984);

Comprehensive learning support services such as academic advising, personal counseling, and support for students with disabilities (Boylan, 2002b; Clark-Thayer and Cole, 2009; Farmer and Barham, 2001; Noel, Levitz, and Kaufmann, 1982).

Activities of learning assistance programs are often quite different in four-year and two-year institutions. Four-year colleges most often select noncredit activities, while two-year colleges are often more comprehensive, especially regarding the offering of developmental courses. Colleges select from the activities that best meet the needs of their particular student profile. A critical success factor of these activities is in understanding the needs of all incoming students. Rather than offering developmental courses, some four-year colleges pursue other learning assistance activities. A major factor with the mandatory nature of some learning assistance activities is based on the research finding that students who most need these services often fail to use them because of a lack of motivation (Dembo and Seli, 2004).

Implementing this cluster of practices requires significant and sustained funding, which is a defining issue for effectively serving students least likely to graduate: first generation, underrepresented in higher education, academically underprepared in one or more content areas, or economically disadvantaged. Students with the least social capital need these essential learning assistance resources to graduate at the same rate as the most privileged students. Learning assistance requires the same funding status given to building new campus facilities, purchasing new high-technology equipment and networking infrastructure, initiating new academic programs, and supporting intercollegiate athletics.

Two-year colleges are not the only ones that offer comprehensive learning assistance services. The University College Learning Center (http://www .bsu.edu/web/learningcenter/) at Ball State University in Muncie, Indiana, offers a comprehensive program. Although Ball State collaborates with local community colleges to provide developmental courses, the institution also offers noncredit services such as academic advising for all first-year students, assistance for students with disabilities, peer tutoring, supplemental instruction study groups, and workshops. Although users of the learning center's services are often less academically prepared than nonusers as measured by ACT and SAT scores, the center's users earn higher GPAs and persist at higher rates than nonusers.

### Critical Instructional Practices

The next group of practices focuses on specific pedagogical choices for learning assistance activities and courses. Critical instruction practices include:

Embedding multiculturalism in instructional activities and curriculum materials (Clark-Thayer and Cole, 2009; Higbee, Lundell, and Duranczyk, 2003);

Using Universal Instructional Design in the course to reduce learning barriers for all students (Clark-Thayer and Cole, 2009; Higbee, 2003);

Using learning communities (Boylan, 2002b; Malnarich and others, 2003);

Using varied instructional methods for diverse students (Boylan, 2002b; Casazza and Silverman, 1996; Clark-Thayer and Cole, 2009; Farmer and Barham, 2001; Higbee, Lundell, and Duranczyk, 2003);

Testing frequently (Boylan, 2002b; Clark-Thayer and Cole, 2009);

Using technology-based delivery systems with moderation (Boylan, 2002b; Clark-Thayer and Cole, 2009; Farmer and Barham, 2001);

Using active learning strategies (Boylan, 2002b; Clark-Thayer and Cole, 2009);

Employing self-paced mastery learning (Boylan, 2002b; Farmer and Barham, 2001; Roueche, Baker, and Roueche, 1984);

Integrating both critical thinking and learning strategies skill instruction and practice in all developmental courses (Boylan, 2002b; Clark-Thayer and Cole, 2009; Farmer and Barham, 2001; Miller, 1999);

Using classroom assessment techniques (Boylan, 2002b; Clark-Thayer and Cole, 2009);

Providing frequent and timely feedback (Boylan, 2002b; Clark-Thayer and Cole, 2009; Farmer and Barham, 2001);

Using cooperative and collaborative learning activities to engage students in learning (Arendale, 2001; Clark-Thayer and Cole, 2009; Casazza and Silverman, 1996);

Introducing activities based on appropriate learning theories (Casazza and Silverman, 1996; Clark-Thayer and Cole, 2009; Miller, 1999).

Although many of these practices are common in college classrooms, the reason they are included here is that most research studies find these practices positively affect all student outcomes. The line between essential academic practices for the general student population and those for students identified as academically underprepared for a particular course becomes blurred, because the same learning activity often benefits both populations. Rather than employing the old approach of customizing instructional design for the class depending on the prevailing academic preparation of students—those identified as academically underprepared or those identified as academic honors students—the new paradigm provides an enriched learning environment for all.

A significant obligation for implementing these practices rests with the faculty members teaching these developmental courses. They must revise the curriculum and pedagogy. As described more fully in the next group of best practices, professional development for teaching faculty is essential for implementing best practices. Faculty members teaching developmental courses often are assigned more credit hours and earn lower salaries than their counterparts teaching college-level courses. It is difficult for them to find time to engage in this work. Many cannot access needed graduate coursework related to learning assistance, and few graduate programs focus on best and emerging practices for teaching undergraduate college students. An overreliance on part-time and adjunct faculty to teach these developmental courses also denies resources needed for change. These instructors have little time, resources, or incentive to pursue professional development, modify the curriculum, and change pedagogical style. The following section on personnel practices addresses this issue.

### Important Personnel Practices

The most essential resources for learning assistance are the quality and competence of people providing services and teaching the courses. Best practices are insufficient unless the institution selects, retains, and supports key staff and faculty members. Several personnel practices are very important to a program's success:

Selecting faculty and staff with formal academic preparation for learning assistance (Clark-Thayer and Cole, 2009; Miller, 1999; Noel, Levitz, and Kaufmann, 1982);

Providing initial training for paraprofessionals by using certified training programs and conducting training over several days before the academic term begins (Arendale, 2001; Clark-Thayer and Cole, 2009; Miller, 1999);

Providing continuous professional development for all learning assistance positions, including part-time and full-time faculty members, paraprofessionals, and staff (Arendale, 2001; Clark-Thayer and Cole, 2009; Miller, 1999);

Designating a lead instructor for each developmental course area to mentor other faculty teaching these courses (Clark-Thayer and Cole, 2009; Roueche, Baker, and Roueche, 1984);

Encouraging faculty members' willing participation in teaching developmental courses (Clark-Thayer and Cole, 2009; Roueche, Baker, and Roueche, 1984);

Observing, supervising, mentoring, and training paraprofessionals such as student tutors and study group facilitators throughout the academic term (Arendale, 2001; Clark-Thayer and Cole, 2009; Miller, 1999);

Involving staff and faculty in professional associations related to learning assistance (Boylan, 2002b; Clark-Thayer and Cole, 2009; Miller, 1999).

Two central themes emerge from these personnel practices. The first is hiring faculty and staff qualified and committed to learning assistance. In the past, the faculty assigned to teach developmental courses were part-time adjuncts or full-time faculty members required to teach the classes as part of their overall teaching load. This practice fails to engender commitment and enthusiasm for teaching these courses among faculty whose preference is teaching other college-level courses.

Hiring decisions and professional development of learning assistance faculty and staff members should be taken as seriously as elsewhere at the institution. The commitment can be demonstrated by considering only applicants with formal training and extensive experience, conducting national searches to fill positions and advertising in relevant regional and national publications, contacting graduate programs producing learning assistance professionals for potential job applicants, and providing time and funds for continued professional development. Continuous professional development is necessary to increase quality and meet emerging needs.

The second theme emerging from these best practices is the need for extensive initial training and ongoing professional development for all learning assistance personnel: student workers, paraprofessional tutors and study group leaders, adjunct faculty members, and full-time staff and faculty members. Significant and sustained professional development is necessary to maintain peak performance and learn new emerging practices.

### Rigorous Evaluation Procedures

Best practices become ineffectual without sustained and comprehensive evaluation. Evaluation renders judgment about the efficacy of current learning assistance services and spurs revision as needed to meet its mission and goals. Evaluation provides essential feedback to modify practices to meet needs. In addition, evaluation studies justify maintaining and even expanding learning assistance. Rigorous evaluation procedures include:

Using rigorous qualitative and quantitative evaluation models (Boylan, 2002b; Clark-Thayer and Cole, 2009; Farmer and Barham, 2001; Miller, 1999);

Adopting national standards in specific areas related to learning assistance such as program administration, new student orientation, TRIO, tutoring, course-based learning assistance programs, and developmental education classes (Clark-Thayer and Cole, 2009; Miller, 1999);

Employing systematic program evaluation regularly and using formative and summative evaluation (Boylan, 2002b; Clark-Thayer and Cole, 2009; Farmer and Barham, 2001; Miller, 1999; Roueche, Baker, and Roueche, 1984);

Revising the learning assistance program based on the results of evaluation (Boylan, 2002b; Farmer and Barham, 2001; Miller, 1999);

Disseminating evaluation reports widely to campus stakeholders and policymakers (Farmer and Barham, 2001; Miller, 1999; Roueche, Baker, and Roueche, 1984).

This group of activities is difficult for many learning assistance personnel for many reasons. Personnel might lack knowledge of and skill with program evaluation protocols, while senior administrators at the institution might not require regular studies. Learning assistance personnel often feel overwhelmed with their workload and do not perceive they possess the time to conduct such studies, do not have a vision for the long-term benefit of such activities, prefer providing immediate service to students, and do not believe the time spent yields significant value.

Learning assistance personnel may need to take two actions to increase their ability to conduct evaluation studies. The first is to complete graduate courses in evaluation to gain the knowledge and skills needed. The second is to seek other campus personnel to help them. Key players could be education faculty with expertise in program evaluation, mathematics faculty who are experts in statistical analysis, staff from the institutional research unit, and personnel from enrollment management services, the registrar's office, or other campus units that have an interest in and access to key information regarding student achievement and persistence.

The competence and skill of learning assistance personnel are essential for implementing best practices and improving programs. As described earlier, hiring competent personnel and providing ongoing professional development are essential practices. Other partners in helping to address provision of professional development are the professional associations representing the field. Although they are excellent at hosting national conferences that provide numerous professional development topics, however, they generally do little to assist with online workshops for program evaluation and other high-demand topics. Of the nearly 70,000 professionals working full or part time in the field of learning assistance, fewer than 5,000 are members of these professional associations. A smaller number have time and resources to attend national conferences hosted by these organizations. One exception is the Association for the Tutoring Profession, which provides inexpensive online Webinars quarterly for professionals to pursue professional development. None of the organizations, however, offer sophisticated and comprehensive online courses, especially in program evaluation. Other professional associations in higher education and other professions already offer considerable online education services such as teleconferences, Webinars, downloadable publications, and other Internet-based services for their members. With the ongoing national budget crisis, funding to attend national conferences is declining for many professionals. National professional associations representing learning assistance professionals must quickly reallocate resources for distance learning of their members, or they may become inaccessible for professionals unable to attend national or even state conferences.

### Necessary Institutional Practices, Policies, and Learning Environment

Enrollment managers often argue that student retention is everyone's business. Involvement by all campus programs is necessary to create a positive learning climate supporting students' persistence to graduation. This group of best practices by institutional leaders places learning assistance in the core of the college. It requires considerable and sustained effort, especially among senior institutional leaders. The campus learning environment is influenced by the decisions and policies of senior management.

Necessary institutional practices, policies, and learning environments include several requirements:

Positioning learning assistance as a campuswide responsibility (McCabe, 2000; Noel, Levitz, and Kaufmann, 1982);

Funding learning assistance through stable institutional resources (Clark-Thayer and Cole, 2009; McCabe, 2000; Miller, 1999; Noel, Levitz, and Kaufmann, 1982);

Adopting standards-based practices rigorously evaluated and validated by external organizations such as the Council for the Advancement of Standards, the College Reading and Learning Association, and the National Association of Developmental Education (Clark-Thayer and Cole, 2009; Miller, 1999);

Managing faculty and student expectations of learning assistance capabilities (Boylan, 2002b);

Sharing successful instructional strategies among campus instructors (Boylan, 2002b; Miller, 1999);

Instituting strong administrative support for learning assistance activities and programs (Clark-Thayer and Cole, 2009; Miller, 1999; Noel, Levitz, and Kaufmann, 1982).

The central theme of these actions is assimilation of learning assistance in the larger campus learning environment. Too often learning assistance operates with little connection and support in the institution. Leaders of the learning assistance programs need the support and mentorship of senior management to assume this central location in the institution. A major challenge is perceived negative stereotypes of learning assistance. No annual national rating services praise the amount of funds expended or number of students admitted who need some form of learning assistance. Instead, schools attracting the best academically prepared students, the largest number of merit award winners, the highest average scores on standardized entrance exams, and the largest external donations garner the limelight and the recognition. Astin (1984, 1985) advocates a paradigm shift of values in higher education. Rather than focusing on what social capital students bring to the institution, the emphasis is shifted to how much students develop while they attend the institution. Perhaps if it were the metric widely reported in the national press, some new institutions would emerge on the top lists, including community colleges.

### Tying Together Standards and Next Steps

Is it necessary to implement all these best practices? It depends on what students' needs are. The place to start is with a careful audit of learning assistance activities on campus. At most institutions, these services are widely distributed and too often poorly coordinated with one another. Before spending any more money on these activities, the first step is to be sure that the money currently spent is being used efficiently and effectively. Conducting a gap analysis identifies what is missing that needs to be added to current services. National standards for the field could be useful as an audit tool (Clark-Thayer and Cole, 2009; Miller, 1999). Visiting peer institutions of similar size and admissions selectivity can provide examples of practices and policies to implement. Once students' needs have been identified, the next step is to establish clear and measurable goals for the learning assistance program. Integrating the program with academic affairs, enrollment management, and student services provides access to needed resources and makes it accountable to each. *Then* it is time to select from the previously identified best practices.

The final part of this report recommends specific actions to deal with the challenges raised by learning assistance personnel, senior-level campus administrators, professional associations, and state and national policymakers.

# The Future of the Field

THROUGHOUT ITS LONG HISTORY in postsecondary education, learning assistance has bridged the gap between students' academic preparation and schools' academic expectations, becoming more sophisticated in its approach. Especially with increasing diversity of the student population, learning assistance must more effectively serve a wider range of student ability groups and support the growing legion of online learners.

A key resource to increase the effectiveness of learning assistance is collaboration with others in the higher education community sharing common goals (Upcraft, Gardner, and Barefoot, 2005). These partners include first-year experience programs, new student orientation, offices of students with disabilities, enrollment management offices, academic advising, counseling services, high school–college bridge, dual-credit high school and college courses, and the like. These potential partners are widely respected, understood, and supported by higher education. Alliances and collaborations with them build credibility, capability, and effectiveness.

This chapter identifies action steps to improve the impact of learning assistance. The first section of the chapter focuses on research identifying best practices for learning assistance activities. The second section provides specific steps for learning assistance professionals, managers of learning assistance centers or departments, upper-level campus administrators, state policymakers, national professional associations related to learning assistance, and federal policymakers. The challenges and needs are so daunting that involvement by all stakeholders is required to improve student achievement and persistence toward graduation. Because learning assistance operates at the crossroads of academic affairs, students affairs, and enrollment management, involvement by all three is mandatory.

# Recommendations for Future Research

As shown earlier, the field has generated limited research. A serious challenge for the field relates to the background and academic resources of professionals providing and managing the services. Many are staff members or non-tenure-track faculty members often lacking resources and time to conduct rigorous research leading to new best practices. Their professional development is essential for them to complete this new research and move the field forward to more effective and cost-effective practices.

### Changes in Learning Assistance Research

Review of the professional literature suggests the field is slow in assessing practices and generating sufficient scholarly studies. This weakness is improving as more professionals return to college and earn terminal degrees that require rigorous research and evaluation skills. They acquire the skills and tools needed for conducting qualitative and quantitative research studies too often lacking in the past. A challenge for producing more quality research is that few of those working in or leading learning assistance programs are tenured or tenure-track faculty members. These faculty members are expected to conduct rigorous research studies and publish in scholarly journals. Through attaining terminal degrees, they gained essential skills for rigorous research studies. As part of their scope of work, they have the necessary time and resources. Too often these resources are unavailable for those working in the field. Often they are student affairs employees with twelve-month contracts and heavy workloads that preclude research activities or learning assistance professionals holding faculty rank with heavy teaching workloads and no provision of release time for research or scholarly writing.

As those tenured faculty members conducting research on learning assistance retire, their positions may be redirected as the senior institutions that commonly employ them eliminate or curtail learning assistance programs. The shift of learning assistance activities from public four-year institutions, especially doctoral-degree granting institutions, to public two-year colleges also influences scholarly research. Faculty members at these institutions often redirect their research to new areas. It will be impossible to replace this research expertise and the resources necessary to conduct it if faculty and staff at two-year institutions with heavy workloads have little recognition or inducement for research and scholarly publications.

The situation is more hopeful for more skilled practitioners and learning assistance managers, however. Several graduate programs focusing on this field prepare administrators and classroom teachers. Previously, the only indirect formal preparation source was degree programs training reading teachers for the secondary level. Grambling State University and National Louis University deliver their learning assistance graduate programs partially or completely online; they serve students throughout the United States. A major new graduate program serving the field is offered through Texas State University–San Marcos. Research skills are a significant and embedded component throughout the degree options. Informal training in evaluation research skills is accessed through membership in research-focused professional societies such as the American Educational Research Association (http://aera.net), American Evaluation Association (http://www.eval.org/), and the Association for Institutional Research (http://airweb.org/). Each of the major professional associations representing the field has increased its conference offerings of research and evaluation sessions. The Council for the Advancement of Standards (http://www.cas.net; Miller, 1999) and the *NADE Self-Evaluation Guides: Models for Assessing Learning Assistance/Developmental Education Programs* (Clark-Thayer and Cole, 2009) serve as national standards for the field and provide rigorous evaluation protocols.

### Areas for Future Research in Learning Assistance

Scholarly research based on previous published research agendas (Boylan, Saxon, Bonham, and Parks, 1993) guide researchers in the field. Following are a few critical issues and questions to investigate. Many are in response to the increasing diversity of the student population.

What are essential elements and components of learning assistance models? With restrictive budgets and limited staff, educators must identify specific activities and components in larger learning assistance–related activities. Identifying the essential components such as a specialized orientation program or a particular tutoring protocol permits redesign of learning assistance approaches for the highest student outcomes with the most efficient delivery system. King, Morris, and Fitz-Gibbon (1987) argue that limiting evaluation to program outcomes potentially answers only the question of whether it works and not the deeper question of what worked and what did not and how those variables contributed to the outcome. "Program implementation research" focuses on the intervention process rather than only the final product. This approach yields valuable information for program revision and improvement. With restrictive budgets common, learning assistance must determine how to improve its efficiency and pare it expenses while achieving desired outcomes for all.

Why is it that some students do not participate? Or if they do participate, do they achieve high outcomes because of involvement in the programs? Learning theories sensitive to individual differences are essential to create new and modify old learning assistance activities. Researchers such as Steel and Graham provide insight through their exploration of complex relationships among academic performance, cultural priorities, and personal identity. Walpole identified interaction and intersection of these identities as creating more challenges for college success. Some students do not avail themselves of opportunities because they do not know how to seek help. Research studies from Dembo and Pintrich identify critical connections between affective and cognitive processes. Research from K–12 education focuses on these areas and is the basis for research with postsecondary students (Dembo and Sali, 2004; Pintrich, 2000). It does no good to add new learning assistance approaches and programs if few avail themselves of them, and of those who do, if they are average to above average in academic preparation.

How does one mainstream best practices of learning assistance into first-year college courses? This question responds to some political leaders' seeking to curtail learning assistance activities for budgetary and philosophical reasons. Others believe these best practices provide a richer and more productive learning experience for all in the class. They learn life-long learning skills essential as workers and as informed citizens. Careful research identifies how to embed these practices into their courses while maintaining academic rigor expected by all. And it is true regardless of content area: humanities, social sciences, and the sciences. Universal Instructional Design presents exciting possibilities but requires more field testing and careful research studies to identify best practices.

A critical area of research and identification of best practices is with developmental courses. This area generates the most criticism of the field of learning assistance. The only national study that took into account variables of how developmental courses were offered is nearly two decades old (Boylan, Bonham, and Bliss, 1994). Other studies have raised doubts about the utility of these courses (Bailey, 2009). For example, a study could be conducted of a national stratified sample of institutions that have been nationally certified for meeting or exceeding national standards for their developmental courses. It could be compared with a similar sample of institutions that have not been certified. Failure to conduct rigorous national studies with this component of learning assistance may provide the excuse for further curtailment of critical services needed for student success.

Finally, how can average educators know which practices are cost-effective and cost-efficient? Presently, no central location exists where one can find a wide collection of carefully researched, evaluated, and validated learning assistance practices. The standards published by the Council for the Advancement of Standards and the National Association for Developmental Education (Clark-Thayer and Cole, 2009) are a positive start. Other scholars publish summaries of best practices. But a central repository of emerging and demonstrated practices rigorously evaluated and validated is necessary with in-depth documentation, sample curricula, and the like. Two examples present a model. The National Diffusion Network of the U.S. Department of Education identified "exemplary educational practices" meeting rigorous standards for improved student outcomes, and other institutions could likely implement the practice. Although the network was eliminated in the early 1990s because of budget cuts, a new incarnation funded by the U.S. Department of Education is the What Works Clearinghouse (http://www.whatworks.ed.gov). The clearinghouse validates and disseminates K–12 educational practices. Expansion of this center or creation of a new one focused exclusively on postsecondary practices is essential.

Assessment and accountability dominate postsecondary education. The field of learning assistance must embrace the challenge and respond accordingly. Not only does the field improve through critical self-evaluation, so do students' achievement and persistence.

# Recommendations for Change

Learning assistance is most effective when it is a campuswide responsibility. It benefits from involvement by a wide array of stakeholders at the institution and beyond. The following recommendations involve stakeholders throughout the education path: learning assistance professionals, learning assistance centers or departments, upper-level campus administrators, state policymakers, national professional associations, and federal policymakers. A coordinated and comprehensive response by these stakeholders activates learning assistance for higher levels of service.

### Learning Assistance Professionals

Members of the learning assistance profession manage learning assistance centers, coordinate tutoring programs, and instruct students. Many professionals received formal academic degrees and training in other disciplines. Professional development is central for many.

Completing a graduate degree or certification program related to learning assistance is an important asset. Obtaining an advanced degree increases skill and knowledge to conduct program assessment and evaluation. Other outcomes include understanding emerging student learning theories, best education practices, student persistence practices and theories, and other scholarship. In addition to building competence with work tasks, graduate education helps to develop networks of other colleagues in the field. These relationships provide expertise and collaboration partners. Joining professional associations like the American Educational Research Association, American Evaluation Association, and Association for Institutional Research allows one to access essential information for program evaluation and improvement.

Obtaining advanced education increases influence with campus stakeholders and policymakers. If a graduate education is not an option, professional associations offer short-term institutes of a week or more. A best practice identified earlier is professional development of learning assistance personnel. Those with twelve-month contracts especially need institutional support. The most important place for the institution to invest is in its employees.

Wide reading of the professional literature exposes learning assistance personnel to student persistence, learning theories, and cognitive psychology. One habit of highly effective people is to "seek first to understand, then to be understood" (Covey, 1989, p. 235). Reading the professional literature read by upper-level administrators provides insights to their mind-set and identifies a common vocabulary for productive conversations with them. Reading institutional annual reports, accrediting agency reports, strategic planning documents, and broad-based publications such as *About Campus, Change Magazine,* and *The Chronicle of Higher Education* highlights recurring themes, institutional priorities, and critical issues. Effective learning assistance leaders increase precision with language describing and promoting campus learning assistance. Using language and concepts familiar to upper-level administrators promotes better understanding of learning assistance reports and budget requests. Establishing a common vocabulary between learning assistance personnel and college leaders improves communication and influence. Aligning learning assistance activities with institutional and state goals increases the likelihood of stable support. Sharing expertise on campus committees such as enrollment management, admissions, and new student orientation strategically positions learning assistance as an institution-wide resource.

### Learning Assistance Centers and Departments

Increased influence and expertise in the classroom, department, and learning center enable improved knowledge and skills. Mangers of these units have capacity for expanded service to a wider campus community through supplemental and enrichment learning for all.

Expanding service returns campuswide learning assistance to the model operating in the 1700s and 1800s. A strategic error was committed when learning assistance quit serving all students and instead focused on only marginalized students with little social capital and prestige. The value-added contribution of learning assistance for all students was lost, contributing to higher dropout rates for invisible "average" students silently withdrawing from the institution without prediction or warning. Expanded service requires pilot tests and acceptance of results by upper-level administrators to receive sustained funding.

Teaming learning assistance staff with core curriculum faculty members to improve pedagogy and strategies incorporating learning strategies into their classes could raise student outcomes. Adoption of practices by these faculty members improves learning for a wider circle of students. Leveraging the assets of competent staff from learning centers to help faculty members integrate these best practices conserves scarce institutional resources by not having to hire more learning assistance personnel to work with students individually. Seeking program certification from the learning assistance professional associations increases the likelihood of higher student outcomes as curricula and pedagogies naturally resulting from the process are revised. Powerful synergy results when learning communities connect developmental courses with those from the core curriculum.

As mentioned earlier, learning assistance professionals have opportunities to share their expertise with others at the institution. Natural subjects for interaction include student retention, student orientation, the high school–college bridge, and curriculum committees. They position learning assistance in the campus core. In recent decades, campus librarians have provided a model for repositioning, as they reinvented themselves as leaders for easy access to digital scholarship and high-tech learning that nurture academic life. Reframing itself as a center for campuswide enrichment, learning assistance is recognized as a strategic and essential member of the campus community.

### Upper-Level Campus Administrators

Learning assistance professionals need support and guidance from upper-level campus administrators. Critical decisions by these administrators improve the ability of learning assistance to improve student outcomes. Requiring the campus learning assistance director to comply with nationally recognized standards and best practices increases accountability and provides feedback that guides improvement. More resources may be allocated when senior management believes learning assistance meets or exceeds national standards.

Aligning learning assistance activities with campus enrollment management can support higher persistence rates. Establishing a campuswide advisory board for the unit promotes buy-in from other campus stakeholders. The board also provides feedback to learning assistance leadership. Appointing learning assistance personnel to key campus committees leverages their expertise by providing another venue to share and collaborate with other units. Hiring learning assistance personnel credentialed for the field is paramount. But after hiring them, continued professional development upgrades their expertise needed for challenges today and tomorrow.

In addition to connecting learning assistance personnel in the college community, building stronger partnerships "upstream" in the education pathway improves the academic preparation of new college applicants. Many institutions established task forces involving college learning assistance personnel and teachers from high schools frequently sending seniors to the institution. The task forces improve alignment of high school exit competencies with skills expected in college courses. The participation of learning assistance personnel in high school–college summer bridge programs can include coteaching classes with high school teachers and providing academic support activities such as tutoring courses in these programs. Another venue for collaboration is with community adult education centers to provide remedial skill development unavailable at the college. These recommendations have a theme of leveraging learning assistance expertise with the wider education community to improve students' success.

### State Policymakers

Reconsidering the potential negative impact of mission differentiation among institutions may warrant policy changes. Students first enrolling at a community college seeking an undergraduate or higher degree are less likely to graduate than those beginning at a four-year institution (Adelman, 2006; Pascarella and Terenzini, 1991, 2005; Tinto, 1993). This situation results from serious challenges with the transfer process despite articulation agreements. Students sometimes exhaust their student financial aid for classes not accepted by the senior institution. Many of these students are place bound because of commitments to family, work, and residence. They cannot commute long distances to complete their degrees.

Eliminating developmental credit courses at four-year institutions becomes an unfunded mandate for local two-year colleges. They absorb the financial cost of serving more students academically underprepared in one or more academic areas. More faculty must be hired and additional instructional space constructed, renovated, or leased for these classes and staff associated with them to meet higher student enrollment in developmental courses. Increased high school graduation requirements have not eliminated or reduced the need for learning assistance. Although the form changes, the need for learning assistance is constant.

With scarce economic resources, conducting experiments with alternative learning assistance services is warranted. For example, some colleges have merged their learning centers with community adult education centers, creating another variation of the earlier academic preparatory academies. Synergy is provided for better service through shared resources to the college students and adults studying for their ABE and GED degrees. In some states, public colleges contract with local community colleges to teach developmental classes on the campus of the senior institution. Community adult education centers and the community colleges serving an increased number of college students require additional funds. Professional development is essential for staff at ABE/GED centers and the community colleges to meet the needs of students. Research studies are required to analyze college students assigned to the community ABE/GED centers originally designed for serving high school dropouts. Careful research must be conducted to understand whether significant stigma attaches itself to students enrolling in developmental courses at these locations. A national task force comprising leaders from college learning assistance programs and adult education programs convened by state or federal government should recommend policy.

### National Professional Associations

A new and expanded professional learning assistance association would serve as a catalyst for bringing together more resources and stakeholders sharing common values for better service of professionals in the field. Learning assistance is one of a few fields represented by half a dozen professional associations. These organizations compete with one another and duplicate services, costing members additional expense. National leaders exhort these professional associations to create a new association with expanded mission and vision (Gardner, 2000).

The American Council for Developmental Education (recently renamed the Council of Learning Assistance and Developmental Education Associations), comprising all major learning assistance professional associations, created the Blue Ribbon Commission to analyze the field and recommend changes (http://blueribboncommission.org). The commission comprised past and current national leaders of those associations. The report by the commission (Blue Ribbon Commission, 2006) examined strengths, weaknesses, opportunities, and threats of the field and the organizations serving it. The report identified three paths of new actions by the organizations: increased coordination among existing associations, more collaborative ventures among the groups, and creation of a new professional association.

> *Creating a new and more inclusive association addresses many of the current weaknesses and threats and provides the best opportunity for future service. The intent would be to build a new organization, not merely a merger. Rather than just consolidating the current membership spread among the existing organizations, the intent would be to become more inclusive and hence attract many more members to this new organization. Rather than dividing leadership, resources, and scholarship among the organizations, all would be centralized within one. This synergy of resources would be a powerful engine for expanded service to current and future members. It would be more cost efficient to the organization members since they can avoid the need to join multiple organizations and travel to the various national conferences or competing state chapter events. This approach would make available to all the unique talents and resources that have previously been distributed among the organizations. There would be a consistent approach to standards and certifications. Having one voice would increase the clarity of the field's position on critical issues with policymakers. We would join most fields in higher education by having one predominant organization that provides a wide suite of services to members. [Blue Ribbon Commission, 2006, p. 7]*

New services by the current organizations or through a new one include online professional development activities, certification programs for individual professionals, advocacy for learning assistance activities, and the like. Many of them are listed in the commission's report, available through the group's Web site. The best solution, however, is to create a new professional association with an expanded vision and mission and more inclusive language. A working group established by the College Reading and Learning Association and the National Association for Developmental Education, both members of the American Council of Developmental Education Associations, convened a commission of former and current national leaders to investigate creation of a new professional association. Their findings were published through professional journals sponsored by both organizations and are being debated currently by members and leaders of these two associations.

## Federal Policymakers

Improved elementary and secondary education has been fostered through national centers for best practices in K–12 education. A similar national center is required for identification, validation, and dissemination of best practices for increasing college access, achievement, and graduation, especially for historically underrepresented students. No federally supported agency is charged with that primary mission, and no comprehensive national database exists of validated activities and programs.

A national center for access and success for postsecondary students funded by the U.S. Department of Education could identify successful educational practices serving students academically underprepared and historically underrepresented in postsecondary education, validate educational practices improving academic performance and graduation rates, award grants to evaluate promising best practices, and disseminate emerging and best practices widely through the Internet and other emerging technologies such as online conferencing, video training modules, downloadable reports and curricula, individual consultations, training workshops, and the like.

Although the U.S. Department of Education disperses nearly $2 billion annually for programs that serve postsecondary students through Title III, Title V, TRIO, and the like, no one identifies, validates, and disseminates best practices solely at the postsecondary level. Traditional dissemination channels of conference presentations and scattered reports in the professional literature fail to provide a one-stop location for practices that have undergone validation deeming them worthy for adoption at postsecondary institutions across the country. Institutions cannot afford the time or potential waste of precious institutional resources implementing programs not validated.

Establishing a national center for access and success for postsecondary students would provide such a one-stop location for information about validated best practices that institutions and state policymakers can trust will make a difference in improving students' academic achievement and persistence, especially for those who are historically underrepresented. This one-stop online service would help users sort through the database of practices and select those that meet their institution's needs. More than a depository of reports, the Web site would provide online conferences, showcases of best practices, technical assistance, video modules for professional development related to student access and success, and assistance for promising practices to be validated and awarded the status of best practice. Finally, the Web site could provide basic information about each practice on how to implement and support it along with the institutional requirements needed for success.

A precedent for the proposed center was managed for several decades in the Department of Education's Office of Educational Research and Improvement (OERI). Within OERI, the Program Effectiveness Panel (PEP) reviewed educational practices. Through rigorous evaluation, emerging practices were "validated" if they demonstrated higher academic performance. These validated practices were then disseminated to the education community. OERI's National Diffusion Network (NDN) awarded grants to a few PEP-certified programs for national dissemination. PEP and NDN were eliminated in the mid-1990s because of widespread budget cuts in the department. The proposed center would increase effectiveness and efficiency by using emerging technologies for the dissemination of information; identify promising practices by inviting Title III, Title IV, TRIO, and Fund for the Improvement of Postsecondary Education grant recipients to apply; identify and test new emerging practices; and fund itself through the Department of Education. Individual institutions would be spared the expense and time of creating programs by instead selecting from a previously validated list of best practices.

# Summary

Learning assistance must transform and reengineer itself through new language, partnerships, objectives, and programs (Gardner, 2000). Current language defines and limits it (Arendale, 2005b; Clowes, 1980; Gardner, 2000; Higbee, 1996; Maxwell, 1997; McGrath and Spear, 1994). New partners create synergy that raises academic achievement and persistence towards graduation (Upcraft, Gardner, and Barefoot, 2005). Learning and student development must be integrated and seamless. The American College Personnel Association and the National Association of Student Personnel Administrators have proclaimed a new transformative learning path. *"Learning Reconsidered* is an argument for the integrated use of all of higher education's resources in the education and preparation of the whole student. It is also an introduction to new ways of understanding and supporting learning and development as intertwined, inseparable elements of the student experience. It advocates for transformative education—holistic process of learning that places the student at the center of the learning experience" (Keeling, 2004, p. 1).

This paradigm guides learning assistance to a more effective and essential role. Mainstreamed learning assistance offers noncredit learning services for all students, integrates developmental courses in learning communities, provides class-based tutoring, supports distance and online learners, embeds best practices of learning assistance in core curriculum courses, and facilitates faculty development services. Best practices promote students' holistic development.

New language, vision, and approaches move the profession forward. Learning assistance operates best at the crossroads of academic affairs, student affairs, and enrollment management. Careful choices at this junction position learning assistance professionals and their stakeholders to foster higher student learning outcomes, increased student persistence to graduation, and fulfillment of institutional mission. Confluence of academic affairs, student affairs, and enrollment management creates a busy intersection of campus needs. Learning assistance belongs here, as many students access and excel through activities and curricular approaches provided by this essential component. Properly funded, resourced, staffed, coordinated, and positioned, learning assistance is a bridge to access at the crossroads of the institution.

# References

Abraham, A. A., and Creech, J. D. (2000). *Reducing remedial education: What progress are states making?* Educational Benchmark 2000 Series. Atlanta: Southern Regional Education Board. Retrieved August 19, 2004, from http://www.sreb.org.

Achieve. (2007a). *Aligned expectations? A closer look at college admissions and placement tests.* Washington, DC: Author. Retrieved April 13, 2007, from http://www.achieve.org/files/ Admissions_and_Placement_FINAL2.pdf.

Achieve. (2007b). *Closing the expectation gap. An annual report. 50-state progress report on the alignment of high school policies with the demands of college and work.* Washington, DC: Achieve. Retrieved April 13, 2007 from, http://www.achieve.org/files/50-state-07-Final.pdf.

Adelman, C. (2004). *Student academic histories in postsecondary education, 1972–2000.* Washington, DC: National Center for Education Statistics, U.S. Department of Education.

Adelman, C. (2006). *The tool box revisited: Paths to degree completion from high school through college.* Washington, DC: U.S. Department of Education. Retrieved February 18, 2009, from http://www.ed.gov/rschstate/research/pubs/toolboxrevisit/toolbox.pdf.

Alphen, S. V. (2009). The educational quality of early school leavers and the cross-national variation of the income disadvantage. *Educational Research and Evaluation, 15*(6), 543–560.

American Psychological Association. (2010). *Publication manual of the American Psychological Association* (6th ed.). Washington, DC: American Psychological Association.

Ancheta, A. N. (2007). Antidiscrimination law and race-conscious recruitment, retention, and financial aid policies in higher education. In G. Orfield, P. Marin, S. M. Flores, and L. M. Garces (Eds.), *Charting the future of college affirmative action: Legal victories, continuing attacks, and new research* (pp. 15–34). Los Angeles: The Civil Rights Project at UCLA.

Anderson, G., Daugherty, E.J.B., and Corrigan, D. M. (2005). The search for a critical mass of minority students: Affirmative action and diversity of highly selective universities and colleges. *The Good Society, 14*(3), 51–57.

Arendale, D. R. (2001). Effect of administrative placement and fidelity of implementation of the model on effectiveness of supplemental instruction programs. Doctoral dissertation,

University of Missouri–Kansas City, 2000. *Dissertation Abstracts International, 62,* 93. ERIC Document Reproduction Service ED 480 590.

Arendale, D. R. (2002a). A memory sometimes ignored: The history of developmental education. *Learning Assistance Review, 7*(1), 5–13.

Arendale, D. R. (2002b). Then and now: The early history of developmental education. *Research & Teaching in Developmental Education, 18*(2), 3–26.

Arendale, D. R. (2004). Mainstreamed academic assistance and enrichment for all students: The historical origins of learning assistance centers. *Research for Education Reform, 9*(4), 3–21.

Arendale, D. R. (Ed.). (2005a). *Postsecondary peer cooperative learning programs annotated bibliography.* Retrieved May 8, 2005 from http://www.tc.umn.edu/~arend011/bibdir.htm.

Arendale, D. R. (2005b). Terms of endearment: Words that help define and guide developmental education. *Journal of College Reading and Learning, 35*(2), 66–82.

Arendale, D. R. (Ed.). (2009). Glossary of essential terms for learning assistance and developmental education. In S. Clark-Thayer and L. P. Cole (Eds.), *NADE self-evaluation guides: Best practice in academic support programs* (2nd ed., pp. 151–171). Clearwater, FL: H&H Publishing.

Arendale, D. R., and Ghere, D. (2008). Teaching history using Universal Instructional Design. In J. L. Higbee and E. Goff (Eds.), *Pedagogy and student services for institutional transformation: Implementing universal design in higher education* (pp. 113–130). Minneapolis: College of Education and Human Development, University of Minnesota.

Arendale, D. R., and others. (2007). A glossary of developmental education and learning assistance terms. *Journal of College Reading and Learning, 38*(1), 10–34.

Astin, A. W. (1984). Student involvement: A developmental theory for higher education. *Journal of College Student Personnel, 25,* 297–308.

Astin, A. W. (1985). *Achieving educational excellence.* San Francisco: Jossey-Bass.

Bailey, T. (2009). Challenge and opportunity: Rethinking the role and function of developmental education in community college. In A. C. Bueschel and A. Venezia (Eds.), *Policies and practices to improve student preparation and success.* New Directions for Community Colleges, no. 145, pp. 11–30. San Francisco: Jossey-Bass.

Barbe, W. (1951). Reading-improvement services in colleges and universities. *School and Society, 74*(1907), 6–7.

Barefoot, B. O. (2003). *Findings from the second national survey of first-year academic practices.* Brevard, NC: Policy Center for the First Year of College. Retrieved July 4, 2004, from http://www.brevard.edu/fyc/survey2002/findings.htm.

Barr, R. B., and Tagg, J. (1995). From teaching to learning: A new paradigm for undergraduate education. *Change Magazine, 27*(6), 13–25.

Bastedo, M. N., and Gumport, P. J. (2003). Access to what? Mission differentiation and academic stratification in U.S. public higher education. *Higher Education, 46*(3), 341–359.

Belfield, C. R., and Levin, H. M. (2007). *The price we pay: Economic and social consequences of inadequate education.* Washington, DC: Brookings Institution.

Blimling, G. S., and Whitt, E. J. (1999). *Good practice in student affairs.* San Francisco: Jossey-Bass.

Blue Ribbon Commission. (2006). *Creating a new vision for the future.* Retrieved April 1, 2006, from http://blueribboncommission.org.

Blumenstyk, G. (2006, March 10). Businesses have remedies for sale, but a cure is not guaranteed: Companies have mixed results in the sale of remedial education. *Chronicle of Higher Education,* B30.

Boesel, D. (1999). *College for all?* Washington, DC: National Library of Education, Office of Educational Research and Improvement, U.S. Department of Education.

Bowen, W. G., Chingos, M. M., and McPherson, M. S. (2009). *Crossing the finish line: Completing college at America's public universities.* Princeton, NJ: Princeton University Press.

Boylan, H. R. (1988). The historical roots of developmental education. Part III. *Review of Research in Developmental Education, 5*(3), 1–3.

Boylan, H. R. (1995a). Making the case for developmental education. *Research in Developmental Education, 12*(2), 1–4.

Boylan, H. R. (1995b). A review of national surveys on developmental education programs. *Research in Developmental Education, 12*(5), 1–6.

Boylan, H. R. (1999). Exploring alternatives to remediation. *Journal of Developmental Education, 22*(3), 2–4.

Boylan, H. R. (2002a). A brief history of the American Council of Developmental Education Associations. In D. B. Lundell and J. L. Higbee (Eds.), *Histories of developmental education* (pp. 11–14). Minneapolis: Center for Research on Developmental Education and Urban Literacy, General College, University of Minnesota.

Boylan, H. R. (2002b). *What works: Research-based best practices in developmental education.* Boone, NC: Continuous Quality Improvement Network with the National Center for Developmental Education.

Boylan, H. R., Bonham, B. S., and Bliss, L. B. (1992). *National study of developmental education: Students, programs and institutions of higher education.* Unpublished manuscript. Boone, NC: National Center for Developmental Education.

Boylan, H. R., Bonham, B. S., and Bliss, L. B. (1994). Who are the developmental students? *Research in Developmental Education, 11*(2), 1–4.

Boylan, H. R., Saxon, D. P., Bonham, B. S., and Parks, H. E. (1993). A research agenda for developmental education: Fifty ideas for future research. *Research in Developmental Education, 10*(3), 1–4.

Boylan, H. R., Saxon, D. P., White, J. R., and Erwin, A. (1994). Retaining minority students through developmental education. *Research in Developmental Education, 11*(3), 1–4.

Boylan, H. R., and White, W. G., Jr. (1987). Educating all the nation's people: The historical roots of developmental education. Part I. *Review of Research in Developmental Education, 4*(4), 1–4.

Brier, E. (1984). Bridging the academic preparation gap: An historical view. *Journal of Developmental Education, 8*(1), 2–5.

Brubacher, J. S., and Rudy, W. (1976). *Higher education in transition: A history of American colleges and universities, 1636–1976* (3rd ed.). New York: Harper & Row.

Burke, P. J. (2002). *Accessing education: Effectively widening participation.* Sterling, VA: Trentham Books.

Canfield, J. H. (1889). *The opportunities of the rural population for higher education.* Nashville: National Council on Education.

Casazza, M. E., and Bauer, L. (2006). *Access, opportunity, and success: Keeping the promise of higher education.* Westport, CT: Praeger.

Casazza, M. E., and Silverman, S. L. (1996). *Learning assistance and developmental education: A guide for effective practice.* San Francisco: Jossey-Bass.

Center for Teaching Excellence. (2009). *Database and web links to teaching and learning centers in the U.S. and in other countries.* Lawrence, KS: Center for Teaching Excellence. Retrieved December 15, 2009, from http://www.cte.ku.edu/cteInfo/resources/websites .shtml.

Chazan, M. (1973). *Compensatory education.* London: Butterworth.

Chickering, A. W., and Gamson, Z. F. (1987). *Seven principles for good practice in undergraduate education.* Washington, DC: American Association for Higher Education. Retrieved April 9, 2005, from http://learningcommons.evergreen.edu/pdf/fall1987.pdf.

Christ, F. L. (1971). Systems for learning assistance: Learners, learning facilitators, and learning centers. In *Fourth annual proceedings of the Western College Reading Association. Volume IV: Interdisciplinary aspects of reading instruction* (pp. 32–41). Los Angeles: Western College Reading Association.

Christ, F. L. (1997). The learning assistance center as I lived it. In S. Mioduski, and G. Enright (Eds.), *Proceedings of the 15th and 16th annual institutes for learning assistance professionals: 1994 and 1995* (pp. 1–14). Tucson: University Learning Center, University of Arizona.

Clark-Thayer, S., and Cole, L. P. (Eds.). (2009). *NADE self-evaluation guides: Best practice in academic support programs.* Clearwater, FL: H&H Publishing.

Clemont, W. K. (1899, February). The Northwestern State University and its preparatory school. *Educational Review, 17,* 154–163.

Clowes, D. A. (1980). More than a definitional problem: Remedial, compensatory, and developmental education. *Journal of Developmental and Remedial Education, 4*(1), 8–10.

Cohen, A. M., and Brawer, F. B. (2002). *The American community college.* (4th ed.). San Francisco: Jossey-Bass.

Congos, D. H., and Schoeps, N. (1998). Inside supplemental instruction sessions: One model of what happens that improves grades and retention. *Research and Teaching in Developmental Education, 15*(1), 47–61.

Continuous Quality Improvement Network and American Productivity and Quality Center. (2000). *Benchmarking best practices in developmental education.* Houston: American Productivity and Quality Center.

Corash, K., and Baker, E. D. (2009). *Calculating the productivity of instruction: Using a simplified cost-benefit analysis to promote effective practice.* Denver: Colorado Community College System. Retrieved January 10, 2009, from http://www.communitycollegecentral.org/ StateInitiatives/Colorado/ColoradoCost_Benefit.pdf.

Council for the Advancement of Standards. (2009). Internet homepage. Retrieved September 25, 2009, from http://www.cas.edu.

Covey, S. R. (1989). *The seven habits of highly effective people: Powerful lessons in personal change.* New York: Simon & Shuster.

Cowie, A. (1936). *Educational problems at Yale College in the eighteenth century.* New Haven, CN: Yale University Press.

Craig, C. M. (1997). *Developmental education: A historical perspective.* Paper presented at the National Association for Developmental Education Annual Conference, Atlanta, GA. Available from C. M. Craig, assistant professor of mathematics in learning support, Augusta State University, 2500 Walton Way, Augusta, GA 30904.

Cross, K. P. (1976). *Accent on learning.* San Francisco: Jossey-Bass.

Curti, M., and Carstensen, V. (1949). *The University of Wisconsin: A History 1848–1925* (Volume 1). Madison: University of Wisconsin Press.

Delta Project. (2009). *Calculating cost-return for investment in student success.* Washington, DC: Delta Project. Retrieved January 10, 2010, from http://www.deltacostproject.org/resources/pdf/ISS_cost_return_report.pdf.

Dembo, M. H., and Seli, H. P. (2004). Students' resistance to change in learning strategies courses. *Journal of Developmental Education, 27*(3), 2–4.

Dempsey, B.J.L. (1985). *An update on the organization and administration of learning assistance programs in U.S. senior institutions of higher education.* ERIC Document Reproduction Service ED 257 334.

Eggleston, L. E., and Laanan, F. S. (2001). Making the transition to the senior institution. In F. S. Laanan (Ed.), *Transfer students: Trends and issues.* New Directions for Community Colleges, no. 114, pp. 87–97. San Francisco: Jossey-Bass.

Enright, G. (1975). College learning skills: Frontierland origins of the learning assistance center. In *Proceedings of the Eighth Annual Conference of the Western College Reading Association: College Learning Skills Today and Tomorrow* (pp. 81–92). Las Cruces, NM: Western College Reading Association. ERIC Document Reproduction Service ED 105 204.

ERIC Clearinghouse on Higher Education. (2001). *Critical issues bibliography (CRIB) sheet: Summary bridge programs.* Washington, DC: ERIC Clearinghouse on Higher Education. ERIC Document Reproduction Service ED 466 854.

Farmer, V. L., and Barham, W. A. (Eds.). (2001). *Selected models of developmental education programs in higher education.* Lanham, MD: University Press of America.

Frost, J., and Rowland, G. (1971). *Compensatory education: The acid test of American education.* Dubuque, IA: William C. Brown.

Fulton, O., and others. (1981). *Access to higher education: Programme of study into the future of higher education.* Surrey, England: Society for Research into Higher Education. ERIC Document Reproduction Service ED 215 603.

Furlong, T., and Fleishman, S. (2000). *College preparatory program agreements between state universities and community colleges: A Level 1 review.* Tallahassee: Florida State Board of Community Colleges. ERIC Document Reproduction Service ED 440 716.

Gardner, J. (2000). The changing roles of developmental educators. *Journal of College Reading and Learning, 31*(1), 5–18.

Goodwin, W. W. (1895). School English. *Nation, 61*, 291–293.

Gordon, E. E., and Gordon, E. H. (1990). *Centuries of tutoring: A history of alternative education in America and Western Europe*. Lanham, MD: University Press of America.

Gose, B. (1997, September 19). Tutoring companies take over remedial teaching at some colleges. *Chronicle of Higher Education*, A44.

Greene, J. P. (2000). *The cost of remedial education: How much Michigan pays when students fail to learn skills. Estimate of the annual economic cost to businesses, colleges, and universities to counteract employees' and students' lack of basic reading, writing, and arithmetic skills.* Midland, MI: Mackinac Center for Public Policy. ERIC Document Reproduction Service ED 451 277.

Grout, J. (2003, January). Milestones of TRIO history, Part 1. *Opportunity Outlook*, 21–27.

Gumport, P. J., and Bastedo, M. N. (2001). Academic stratification and endemic conflict: Remedial education policy at CUNY. *Review of Higher Education, 24*(4), 333–349.

Hamrick, F. A., Evans, J. J., and Schuh, J. H. (2002). *Foundations of student affairs practice: How philosophy, theory, and research strengthen educational outcomes*. San Francisco: Jossey-Bass.

Hankin, J. N. (Ed.). (1996). *The community college: Opportunity and access for America's first-year students*. Monograph Series No. 19. Columbia: National Resource Center for the First-Year Experience and Students in Transition, University of South Carolina.

Hashway, R. M. (1988). *Foundations of developmental education*. New York: Praeger.

Henderson, D. D., Melloni, B. J., and Sherman, J. G. (1971). *What a learning resource center (LRC) could mean for Georgetown University.* Unpublished manuscript. ERIC Document Reproduction Service ED 055 417.

Higbee, J. L. (1996). Defining developmental education: A commentary. In J. L. Higbee and P. L. Dwinell (Eds.). *Defining developmental education: Theory, research, and pedagogy* (pp. 63–66). Carol Stream, IL: National Association for Developmental Education.

Higbee, J. L. (Ed.). (2003). *Curriculum transformation and disability: Implementing universal design in higher education*. Minneapolis: Center for Research on Developmental Education and Urban Literacy, General College, University of Minnesota.

Higbee, J. L. (2005). Developmental education. In M. L. Upcraft, J. N. Gardner, and B. O. Barefoot (Eds.). *Challenging and supporting the first-year student: A handbook for improving the first year of college* (pp. 292–307). San Francisco: Jossey-Bass.

Higbee, J. L., Arendale, D. R., and Lundell, D. B. (Eds.). (2005). Using theory and research to improve access and retention in developmental education. In C. A. Kozeracki (Ed.), *Responding to the challenges of developmental education* (pp. 5–15). New Directions for Community Colleges, no. 129. San Francisco: Jossey-Bass.

Higbee, J. L., and Dwinell, P. L. (Eds.). (1998). *Developmental education: Preparing successful college students*. Monograph Series No. 24. Columbia: National Resource Center for the First-Year Experience and Students in Transition, University of South Carolina.

Higbee, J. L., and Goff, E. (Eds.). (2008). *Pedagogy and student services for institutional transformation: Implementing universal design in higher education*. Minneapolis: Regents of the

University of Minnesota, Center for Research on Developmental Education and Urban Literacy, College of Education and Human Development, University of Minnesota.

Higbee, J. L., Lundell, D. B., and Arendale, D. R. (Eds.). (2005). *The General College vision: Integrating intellectual growth, multicultural perspectives, and student development.* Minneapolis: Center for Research on Developmental Education and Urban Literacy, General College, University of Minnesota.

Higbee, J. L., Lundell, D. B., and Duranczyk, I. M. (Eds.). (2003). *Multiculturalism in developmental education.* Annual Monograph Series No. 4. Minneapolis: Center for Research on Developmental Education, General College, University of Minnesota.

Higher Education Funding Council for England. (2006). *Widening participation: A review.* London: Higher Education Funding Council for England.

Hill, A. S. (1885, June). English in our schools. *Harper's Magazine,* 123–133.

Hodges, R. Dochen, C. W., and Donna, J. (2001). Increasing students' success: When supplemental instruction becomes mandatory. *Journal of College Reading and Learning, 31*(2), 143–156.

Horn, L. J., Chen, X., and MPR Associates. (1998). *Toward resiliency: At-risk students who make it to college.* Washington, DC: Office of Educational Research and Improvement, U.S. Department of Education.

Hultgren, D. D. (1970). The role of the individual learning center in effecting educational change. In G. B. Schick and M. M. May (Eds.), *Reading: Process and pedagogy.* 19th National Conference Yearbook (Volume 2, pp. 89–94). Milwaukee: National Reading Conference.

Ignash, J. M. (Ed.). (1997). *Implementing effective policies for remedial and developmental education.* New Directions for Community Colleges, no. 100. San Francisco: Jossey-Bass.

Jehangir, R. R. (2002). Higher education for whom? The battle to include developmental education at the four-year university. In J. L. Higbee, D. B. Lundell, and I. M. Duranczyk (Eds.), *Developmental education: Policy and practice* (pp. 17–34). Auburn, GA: National Association for Developmental Education.

Jenkins, D., Jaggars, S. S., and Roksa, J. (2009). *Promoting gatekeeper course success among community college students needing remediation: Findings and recommendations from a Virginia study.* New York: Community College Research Center, Teachers College, Columbia University. Retrieved January 5, 2010, from http://ccrc.tc.columbia.edu/Publication.asp?/UID=714.

Jeynas, W. (2007). *American educational history: School, society, and the common good.* Thousand Oaks, CA: Sage.

Johnsrud, L. K. (2000). Higher education staff: Bearing the brunt of cost containment. In *NEA 2000 almanac of higher education* (pp. 101–118). Washington, DC: National Education Association.

Kammen, M. (1997). *In the past lane: Historical perspectives on American culture.* New York: Oxford University Press.

Keeling, R. P. (Ed.). (2004). *Learning reconsidered: A campuswide focus on the student experience.* Washington, DC: American College Personnel Association and National Association of

Student Affairs Administrators. Retrieved January 29, 2005 from http://www.myacpa.org/pub/documents/LearningReconsidered.pdf.

Keimig, R. T. (1983). *Raising academic standards: A guide to learning improvement.* ASHE-ERIC Higher Education Research Report, no. 4. Washington, DC: Association for the Study of Higher Education.

Kerstiens, G. (1972). The ombudsman function of the college learning center. In F. Greene (Ed.), *College reading: Problems and programs of junior and senior colleges. 21st National Reading Conference Yearbook* (Volume 2, pp. 221–227). Milwaukee: National Reading Conference.

Kerstiens, G. (1997). Taxonomy of learning support services. In S. Mioduski, and G. Enright (Eds.), *Proceedings of the 15th and 16th annual institutes for learning assistance professionals: 1994 and 1995* (pp. 48–51). Tucson: University Learning Center, University of Arizona.

King, J. A., Morris, L. L., and Fitz-Gibbon, C. T. (1987). *How to assess program implementation.* Newbury Park, CA: Sage.

Koos, L. V. (1924). *The junior college.* Minneapolis: University of Minnesota.

Koski, W. S., and Levin, H. M. (1998). *Replacing remediation with acceleration in higher education: Preliminary report on literature review and initial interviews.* Stanford, CA: National Center for Postsecondary Improvement. Retrieved July 1, 2004, from http://www.stanford.edu/group/ncpi/documents/pdfs/4-01_remediation.pdf.

Kozol, J. (1991). *Savage inequalities: Children in America's schools.* New York: Crown Publishers.

Kulik, C. C., Kulik, J. A., and Schwalb, B. J. (1983). College programs for high-risk and disadvantaged students: A meta-analysis of findings. *Review of Educational Research, 53*(3), 397–414.

Kulik, J. A., and Kulik, C.-L. C. (1991). *Developmental instruction: An analysis of the research.* Boone, NC: National Center for Developmental Education, Appalachian State University.

Lazerson, M., Wagener, U., and Shumanis, N. (2000). Teaching and learning in higher education, 1980–2000. *Change, 32*(3), 12–19.

Lederman, M. J., Ryzewic, S. R., and Ribaudo, M. (1983). *Assessment and improvement of the academic skills of entering freshmen: A national survey.* Research Monograph Series, Report No. 5. New York: Instructional Resource Center, Office of Academic Affairs, City University of New York.

Lucas, C. J. (2006). *American higher education: A history.* New York: Palgrave Macmillan.

Lundell, D. B., and Higbee, J. L. (Eds.). (2001). *Theoretical perspectives for developmental education.* Annual Monograph Series No. 1. Minneapolis: Center for Research on Developmental Education and Urban Literacy, General College, University of Minnesota.

Lundell, D. B., and Higbee, J. L. (Eds.). (2002). *Histories of developmental education.* Annual Monograph Series No. 2. Minneapolis: Center for Research on Developmental Education and Urban Literacy, General College, University of Minnesota.

Lyall, K. C., and Sell, K. R. (2006). The de facto privatization of American public higher education. *Change Magazine, 38*(1), 4–13.

Malnarich, G., and others. (2003). *The pedagogy of possibilities: Developmental education, college-level studies, and learning communities.* National Learning Communities Project

Monograph Series. Olympia, WA: Washington Center for Improving the Quality of Undergraduate Education, Evergreen State College, with the American Association for Higher Education.

Manzo, K. K. (2007). Students take more demanding courses: Scores on national tests show no improvement. *Education Week, 26*(25). Retrieved February 28, 2007, from http://www .edweek.org/we/articles/2007/02/23/25naep.h26.html.

Martin, D. C., and Arendale, D. R. (1997). *Review of research concerning the effectiveness of supplemental instruction from the University of Missouri–Kansas City and other institutions from across the United States.* Unpublished manuscript, University of Missouri–Kansas City. ERIC Document Reproduction Service ED 370 502.

Martinez, S., Snider, L. A., and Day, E. (2003). *Remediation in higher education: A review of the literature.* Topeka: Kansas State Board of Education. Retrieved July 1, 2004, from http://www.ksde.org/pre/postsecondary_remediation.doc.

Maryland Higher Education Commission. (1997). *Study of the effectiveness of "privatizing" remedial services.* Annapolis: Maryland Higher Education Commission. Retrieved February 9, 2007, from http://www.mhec.state.md.us/publications/research/1997Studies/StudyofThe EffectivenessofPrivatizingRemedialServices.pdf.

Maxwell, M. (1979). *Improving student learning skills: A comprehensive guide to successful practices and programs for increasing the performance of underprepared students.* San Francisco: Jossey-Bass.

Maxwell, M. (1997). *Improving student learning skills: A new edition.* Clearwater, FL: H&H Publishing Company.

McCabe, R. H. (2000). *No one to waste: A report to public decision-makers and community college leaders.* Washington, DC: American Association of Community Colleges, Community College Press.

McCabe, R. H. (2003). *Yes we can: A community college guide for developing America's underprepared.* Phoenix, AZ: League for Innovation in the Community College and American Association of Community Colleges.

McCabe, R. H., and Day, P. R. (Eds.). (1998). *Developmental education: A twenty-first-century social and economic imperative.* Washington, DC: League for Innovation in the Community College and The College Board. ERIC Document Reproduction Service ED 421 176.

McGrath, D., and Spear, M. B. (1994). The remediation of the community college. In J. L. Ratcliff, S. Schwarz, and L. H. Ebbers (Eds.). *Community colleges* (pp. 217–228). Needham Heights, MA: Simon & Schuster.

McLure, G. T., and Child, R. L. (1998). Upward bound students compared to other college-bound students: Profiles of nonacademic characteristics and academic achievement. *Journal of Negro Education, 67*(4), 346–363.

McPherson, M. S., and Schapiro, M. O. (1999). *Reinforcing stratification in American higher education: Some disturbing trends.* Stanford, CA: National Center for Postsecondary Improvement, School of Education, Stanford University. Retrieved August 1, 2005, from http://www.stanford.edu/group/ncpi/documents/pdfs/3—02_disturbingtrends.pdf.

Mercer, D. M. (2002). *Synchronous communication in collaborative online learning: Learners' perspectives*. Unpublished Ph.D. dissertation, University of Toronto, Canada.

Miksch, K. L. (2005). Unequal access to college preparatory classes: A critical civil rights issue. In *Brown v. Board of Education: Its impact on public education 1954–2004* (pp. 227–248). New York: Thurgood Marshall Scholarship Fund.

Miksch, K. L. (2008). Widening the river: Challenging unequal schools in order to contest Proposition 209. *Chicana/o Latina/o Law Review, 27*, 111–147.

Miller, T. K. (Ed.). (1999). *The book of professional standards for higher education*. Washington, DC: Council of the Advancement of Standards in Higher Education.

Muraskin, L. (1997). *"Best practices" in student support services: A study of five exemplary sites*. Washington, DC: U.S. Department of Education. ERIC Document Reproduction Service ED 416 784.

National Center for Education Statistics. (1985). *College-level remedial education in the fall of 1983*. Washington, DC: Office of Educational Research and Improvement, U.S. Department of Education.

National Center for Education Statistics. (1991). *College-level remedial education in the fall of 1989*. Washington, DC: Office of Educational Research and Improvement, U.S. Department of Education.

National Center for Education Statistics. (1993). *120 years of American education: A statistical portrait*. Washington, DC: Office of Educational Research and Improvement, U.S. Department of Education.

National Center for Education Statistics. (1996). *Remedial education at higher education institutions in Fall 1995*. Washington, DC: Office of Educational Research and Improvement, U.S. Department of Education.

National Center for Education Statistics. (2003). *Remedial education at degree-granting postsecondary institutions in Fall 2000*. Washington, DC: U.S. Department of Education. Retrieved from http://nces.ed.gov/pubs2004/2004010.pdf.

National Center for Education Statistics (NCES). (2005). *First-generation students in postsecondary education: A look at their college transcripts*. Washington, D.C.: U.S. Department of Education, Author. Retrieved February 18, 2009 from http://nces.ed.gov/pubs2005/2005171.pdf.

Nealy, M. (2009, June 10). Students rally at U.S. Capitol to urge increased support of TRIO and GEAR UP programs. *Issues in Higher Education*. Retrieved December 20, 2009, from http://diverseeducation.com/artman/publish/article_12627.shtml.

Noel-Levitz Center. (2010). *Database of past national award winners of exemplary student retention programs*. Retrieved January 5, 2010, from https://www.noellevitz.com/Papers+and+Research/Retention+Excellence+Awards/.

Noel, L., Levitz, R., and Kaufmann, J. (1982). Campus services for academically underprepared students. In L. Noel, and R. Levitz (Eds.), *How to succeed with academically underprepared students*. Iowa City: ACT National Center for Advancement of Educational Practices.

Ntuk-Iden, M. (1978). *Compensatory education*. Westmead, England: Teakfield Limited.

Oudenhoven, B. (2002). Remediation at the community college: Pressing issues, uncertain solutions. In T. H. Bers and H. D. Calhoun (Eds.), *New steps for the community college*. New Directions for Community Colleges, no. 117. San Francisco: Jossey-Bass.

Parr, E. W. (1930, April). The extent of remedial reading work in state universities in the United States. *School and Society, 31*(799), 547–548.

Pascarella, E. T., and Terenzini, P. T. (1991). *How college affects students*. San Francisco: Jossey-Bass.

Pascarella, E. T., and Terenzini, P. T. (2005). *How college affects students. Volume 2, A third decade of research*. San Francisco: Jossey-Bass.

Payne, E. M., and Lyman, B. G. (1996). Issues affecting the definition of developmental education. In J. L. Higbee, and P. L. Dwinell (Eds.), *Defining developmental education: Theory, research, and pedagogy* (pp. 11–20). Carol Stream, IL: National Association for Developmental Education.

Pedelty, M. H. (2001). Stigma. In J. L. Higbee, D. B. Lundell, and I. M. Duranczyk (Eds.), *2001: A developmental odyssey*. Warrensburg, MO: National Association for Developmental Education.

Perin, D. (2006). Can community colleges protect both access and standards? The problem of remediation. *Teachers College Record, 108*(3), 339–373.

Perkins, R., Kleiner, B., Roey, S., and Brown, J. (2004). *The high school transcript study: A decade of change in curricula and achievement, 1990–2000*. Washington, DC: National Center for Education Statistics, U.S. Department of Education.

Phipps, R. (1998). *College remediation: What it is, what it costs, what's at stake*. Washington, DC: Institute for Higher Education Policy. Retrieved March 1, 2004, from http://www.ihep.com.

Pintrich, P. R. (2000). The role of goal orientation in self-regulated learning. In M. Boekaerts, P. R. Pintrich, and M. Zeldner (Eds.), *Handbook on self-regulation* (pp. 451–502). San Diego: Academic Press.

Piper, J. (1998). An interview with Martha Maxwell. *Learning Assistance Review, 3*(1), 32–39.

Rice, P. (1980). The quality of language and thought in developmental education. *Journal of Developmental and Remedial Education, 4*(1), 9–10.

Richardson, J.T.E., and King, E. (1998). Adult students in higher education: Burden or boom? *Journal of Higher Education, 69*(1), 65–88.

Richardson, R., Martens, K., and Fisk, E. (1981). *Functional literacy in the college setting* AAHE/ERIC Higher Education Research Report, no. 3. Washington, DC: American Association for Higher Education.

Roberts, J. (2009). *A mixed methods study of secondary distance-learning students: Exploring learning styles*. Unpublished Ed.D. dissertation, Walden University, Minnesota.

Roueche, J. E., Baker, G. A., and Roueche, S. D. (1984). *College responses to low-achieving students: A national study*. Orlando: Harcourt, Brace, Jonavich Media.

Roueche, J. E., and Roueche, S. D. (1993). *Between a rock and a hard place: The at-risk student in the open-door college*. Washington, DC: American Association of Community Colleges, Community College Press.

Roueche, J. E., and Roueche, S. D. (1999). *High stakes, high performance: Making remedial education work*. Washington, DC: American Association of Community Colleges, Community College Press.

Roueche, J. E., and Snow, J. G. (1977). *Overcoming learning problems*. San Francisco: Jossey-Bass.

Rubin, M. (1987). What's in a name: The need for resolution of terminology confusion in developmental education. *Journal of College Reading and Learning, 20*(1), 8–15.

Rubin, M. (1991). A glossary of developmental education terms compiled by the CRLA Task Force on Professional Language for College Reading and Learning. *Journal of College Reading and Learning, 23*(2), 1–14.

Rudolph, F. (1956). *Mark Hopkins and the log*. New Haven, CN: Yale University Press.

Rudy, W. (1996). *The campus and a nation in crisis: From the American revolution to Vietnam*. Cranbury, NJ: Associated University Press.

Sandvik, T. (2007). *Contextual understandings in the asynchronous online environment: Writing student' responses to online tutoring*. Unpublished M.A. thesis, University of Alaska–Anchorage.

Sawaan, S. (2006). *Studying the implications of hidden learning styles by tracing learners' behaviors in an e-learning system*. Unpublished M.S. thesis, University of Louisville.

Saxon, D. P., and Boylan, H. R. (2001). The cost of remedial education in higher education. *Journal of Developmental Education, 25*(2), 2–8.

Scott, S. S., McGuire, J. M., and Shaw, S. F. (2003). Universal design for instruction: An approach for inclusion. *Remedial and Special Education, 31*(2), 369–379.

Scrivener, S., and others. (2008). *A good start: Two-year effects of a freshmen learning community program at Kingsborough Community College*. New York: MDRC. Retrieved February 14, 2009, from http://www.mdrc.org/publications/473/full.pdf.

Segal, G. F. (Ed.). (2004). *Annual privatization report 2004*. Washington, DC: Reason Public Policy Institute. Retrieved January 30, 2007, from http://www.reason.org/apr2004/Anpr2004.pdf.

Seymour, E., and Hewitt, N. M. (1997). *Talking about leaving: Why undergraduates leave the sciences*. Boulder, CO: Westview Press.

Shedd, C. (1932). Higher education in the United States. In W. M. Kotschnig and E. Prys (Eds.), *The university in a changing world: A symposium* (pp. 125–162). London: Oxford University Press.

Silver, D., Bourke, A., and Strehorn, K. C. (1998). Universal instructional design in higher education: An approach for inclusion. *Equity & Excellence in Education, 31*(2), 47–51.

Slaughter, S., and Rhoades, G. (2004). *Academic capitalism and the new economy: Markets, state, and higher education*. Baltimore: Johns Hopkins University Press.

Soliday, M. (2002). *The politics of remediation: Institutional and student needs in higher education*. Pittsburgh: University of Pittsburgh Press.

Stahl, N. A., and King, J. R. (2009). A history of college reading. In R. F. Flippo and D. C. Caverly (Eds.), *Handbook of college reading and study strategy research* (2nd ed., pp. 3–25). New York: Routledge.

Stahl, N. A., Simpson, M. L., and Hayes, C. G. (1992). Ten recommendations from research for teaching high-risk college students. *Journal of Developmental Education,16*(1), 2–4.

Swail, W. S. (2004). *Value added: The costs and benefits of college preparatory programs.* American Higher Education Report Series. Washington, DC: Education Policy Institute. Retrieved February 20, 2007, from http://www.educationpolicy.org/pdf/value_added.pdf.

Swail, W. S., and Perna, L. W. (2002). Precollege outreach programs: A national perspective. In W. G. Tierney and L. S. Hagedorn (Eds.), *Increasing access to college* (pp. 15–34). Albany: State University of New York Press.

Swail, W. S., and Roth, D. (2000). The role of early intervention in education reform. *ERIC Review, 8*(1), 3–18. Retrieved December 20, 2009, from http://www.educationalpolicy .org/pdf/ERIC%20Review.pdf.

Thomas, L., Quinn, J., Slack, K., and Casey, L. (2003). *Effective approaches to retaining students in higher education: Directory of practice.* Stoke-on-Trent, U.K.: Institute for Access Studies, Staffordshire University. Retrieved January 31, 2005, from http://www.staffs.ac .uk/institutes/access/docs/Directory1.pdf.

Tinto, V. (1993). *Leaving college: Rethinking the causes and cures of student attrition.* Chicago: University of Chicago Press.

Tinto, V. (1998). *Learning communities and the reconstruction of remedial education in higher education.* Unpublished manuscript. Syracuse, NY: Syracuse University. Retrieved December 15, 2009, from http://z.umn.edu/tintodelc.

Tomlinson, L. M. (1989). *Postsecondary developmental programs: A traditional agenda with new imperatives.* ASHE-ERIC Higher Education Report, no. 3. Washington, DC: School of Education and Human Development, George Washington University.

Townsend, B. K., and Dougherty, K. J. (Eds.). (2007). *Community college missions in the 21st century.* New Directions for Community Colleges, no. 136. San Francisco: Jossey-Bass.

Treisman, P. U. (1986). A study of the mathematics performance of black students at the University of California, Berkeley. Dissertation, University of California, Berkeley, 1985. *Dissertation Abstracts International, 47*(05), 1641.

Universities and Colleges Admission Service. (2003a). *Homepage.* Retrieved January 31, 2005, from http://www.ucas.com/access/.

Universities and Colleges Admission Service. (2003b). *Questions asked by higher education admissions staff.* Retrieved January 31, 2005, from http://www.ucas.com/ucc/access/ ewni/staff.html.

Upcraft, M. L., Gardner, J. N., and Barefoot, B. O. (Eds.). (2005). *Challenging and supporting the first-year student: A handbook for improving the first year of college.* San Francisco: Jossey-Bass.

Valeri-Gold, and others. (1997). Reflection: Experience commentaries by urban developmental studies students. In J. L. Higbee, and P. L. Dwinell (Eds.), *Developmental education: Enhancing student retention* (pp. 3–18). Carol Stream, IL: National Association for Developmental Education.

Vaughan, G. B. (Ed.). (1983). *Issues for community college leaders in a new era.* San Francisco: Jossey-Bass.

Walpole, M. (2007). *Economically and educationally challenged students in higher education: Access to outcomes.* ASHE Higher Education Report, volume 33, number 3. San Francisco: Jossey-Bass.

Weidner, H. Z. (1990). *Back to the future.* Paper presented at the annual meeting of the Conference on College Composition and Communication, Chicago. ERIC Document Reproduction Service ED 319 045.

Weinstein, C., Goetz, E. T., and Alexander, P. A. (Eds.). (1988). *Learning and study strategies: Issues in assessment, instruction, and evaluation.* San Diego: Academic Press.

White, W. G., Jr., and Schnuth, M. L. (1990). College learning assistance centers: Places for learning. In R. M. Hashway (Ed.), *Handbook of developmental education* (pp. 155–177). New York: Praeger.

Williams, P. B. (2005). *On-demand tutoring in distance education: Intrinsically motivated, scalable interpersonal interaction to improve achievement, completion, and satisfaction.* Unpublished Ph.D. dissertation, Brigham Young University, Provo, Utah.

Wilson, A. L. (1993). *The promise of situated cognition.* New Directions for Adults and Continuing Education, no. 57. San Francisco: Jossey-Bass.

Wilson, R., and Justiz, M. (1988). Minorities in higher education: Confronting a time bomb. *Educational Record, 68,* 9–10.

Wright, D. A., and Cahalan, M. W. (1985). *Remedial/developmental studies in institutions of higher education policies and practices.* Paper presented at the Annual Conference of the American Educational Research Association, Chicago. ERIC Document Reproduction Service ED 263 828.

Wyatt, M. (1992). The past, present, and future need for college reading courses in the U.S. *Journal of Reading, 36*(1), 10–20.

# Name Index

## A

Abraham, A. A., 16
Achieve, 76, 77
Adelman, C., 20, 66
Alexander, P. A., 89
Alphen, S. V., 62
Ancheta, A. N., 14
Anderson, G., 20
Arendale, D. R., 8, 9, 10, 11, 12, 13, 23, 24, 42, 72, 73, 75, 76, 83, 88, 89, 90, 92, 94, 96, 98, 99, 100, 118
Astin, A. W., 90, 104

## B

Bailey, T., 69
Baker, E. D., 62
Baker, G. A., 91, 96, 98, 100, 101, 109
Barbe, W., 35
Barefoot, B. O., 12, 59, 60, 67, 105
Barham, W. A., 84, 93, 96, 98, 101
Barr, R. B., 52
Bastedo, M. N., 19
Bauer, L., 22
Belfield, C. R., 15
Blimling, G. S., 88
Bliss, L. B., 14, 15, 18, 35, 66, 68, 69, 73, 92, 109
Blumenstyk, G., 47, 48, 78
Boesel, D., 18
Bonham, B. S., 14, 15, 18, 35, 66, 68, 69, 73, 92, 107, 109
Bourke, A., 83, 90

Bowen, W. G., 3, 15
Boylan, H. R., 4, 14, 15, 16, 18, 21, 25, 35, 41, 45, 48, 59, 60, 61, 66, 68, 69, 71, 73, 78, 80, 84, 91, 92, 94, 96, 98, 100, 101, 103, 107, 109
Brawer, F. B., 17, 40, 67
Brier, E., 16, 27, 29, 32
Brown, J., 20
Brubacher, J. S., 8, 29, 33, 34
Burke, P. J., 12, 46

## C

Cahalan, M. W., 58, 59, 61
Canfield, J. H., 8, 29
Carstensen, V., 29
Casazza, M. E., 22, 26, 29, 41, 45, 93, 98
Casey, L., 45
Center, 71, 74, 84, 92
Chazan, M., 36
Chen, X., 41
Chickering, A. W., 87
Child, R. L., 65
Chingos, M. M., 3, 15
Chipman, Clark, 49
Christ, F. L., 42, 43, 72
Clark-Thayer, S., 92, 94, 96, 97, 98, 99, 100, 101, 103, 104, 109
Clemont, W. K., 29
Clowes, D. A., 10, 32, 36, 37, 38, 118
Cohen, A. M., 17, 40, 67
Cole, L. P., 92, 94, 96, 97, 98, 99, 100, 101, 103

## L

Laanan, F. S., 18
Lazerson, M., 52
Lederman, M. J., 58, 59, 61
Levin, H. M., 15, 84, 92
Levitz, R., 91, 96, 99, 103
Lucas, C. J., 8
Lundell, D. B., 8, 12, 13, 75, 88, 89, 90, 91, 93, 97, 98
Lyall, K. C., 47
Lyman, B. G., 10

## M

Malnarich, G., 73, 75, 92, 98
Manzo, K. K., 20
Martens, K., 34
Martin, D. C., 73
Martinez, S., 12
Maxwell, M., 8, 31, 33, 34, 37, 71, 118
McCabe, R. H., 4, 5, 21, 40, 62, 71, 74, 84, 92, 93, 94, 96, 103
McGrath, D., 17, 118
McGuire, J. M., 83
McLure, G. T., 65
McPherson, M. S., 3, 15, 20
Melloni, B. J., 44
Mercer, D. M., 79
Miksch, K. L., 14, 15
Miller, T. K., 92, 94, 96, 98, 99, 100, 101, 103, 104
Mitchem, Arnold, 49
Morris, L. L., 108
MPR Associates, 41
Muraskin, L., 93

## N

Nealy, M., 38
Noel, L., 91, 96, 99
Ntuk-Iden, M., 37

## O

Oudenhoven, B., 17

## P

Parks, H. E., 69, 107
Parr, E. W., 34

Pascarella, E. T., 17, 65, 113
Payne, E. M., 10
Pedelty, M. H., 10, 12
Perin, D., 17
Perkins, R., 20
Perna, L. W., 65
Phipps, R., 61, 62
Pintrich, P. R., 89, 108
Piper, J., 52

## Q

Quinn, J., 45

## R

Rhoades, G., 19
Ribaudo, M., 58, 59, 61
Rice, P., 10
Richardson, J. T. E., 20
Richardson, R., 34
Roberts, J., 70
Roey, S., 20
Roksa, J., 63, 70
Roth, D., 38
Roueche, J. E., 5, 41, 67, 69, 91, 96, 98, 100, 101
Roueche, S. D., 5, 41, 67, 69, 91, 96, 98, 100, 101
Rowland, G., 37
Rubin, M., 11, 32
Rudolph, F., 26
Rudy, W., 8, 29, 30, 33, 34
Ryzewic, S. R., 58, 59, 61

## S

Sandvik, T., 79
Sawaan, S., 79
Saxon, D. P., 16, 18, 61, 69, 107
Schapiro, M. O., 20
Schnuth, M. L., 42
Schoeps, N., 73
Schuh, J. H., 88
Schwalb, B. J., 67, 69
Scott, S. S., 83
Scrivener, S., 70
Segal, G. F., 78
Seli, H. P., 73, 97, 108

# Subject Index

Britain/United Kingdom: access programs in, 45–47
Bucknell University, 30
Budgets for learning assistance programs, 21

## C

Campus administrators: change recommendations for, 112–113
Campus learning centers, 71–72
Categories of best practices, 93
Categorization of approaches to learning assistance, 64
Center for Educational Advancement, 56
Center for Learning and Teaching (Cornell University), 53
Center for Teaching Excellence, 52
Center for Teaching and Learning (Stanford University), 53
Challenges/controversies: access/opportunity, 21–22; financial, 18–21; lack of knowledge about learning assistance, 7–9; shifting values and perceptions, 9–18; stigma issues, 7
*Change Magazine*, 111
Change recommendations, 110–117
Changes in learning assistance research, 106–110
Chronicle of Higher Education, 111
City University of New York, 70
Civil Rights Act, 36
Civil rights issues, 13–16
Collaboration, 95, 105, 115
College articulation, 76–77
College Board: creation of, 21
College preparatory programs, 15; institutions offering, 33
College Reading and Learning Association (CRLA), 48–49, 116
Columbia College Chicago, 47
Columbia University, 33
Community College of Denver, 56, 62
Community colleges, 17; developmental course access, 19–20; historical role of, 39–42; mission of, 33; preparation of entering students to, 41
Compensatory education, 36–39
Composition of populations of institutions, 30; subpopulations, 9

Concurrent learning experiences approach, 70–76
Concurrent skills acquisition approach, 91–92
Conditional admissions, 32
Conference on College Composition and Communication, 50
Consolidated programs, 95
Continuous Quality Improvement Network and American Productivity and Quality, 71, 74, 84, 92
Coordinated programs: with target classes, 73–75
Cornell University, 53
Cost estimates for providing learning assistance, 61–62
Cost-effective programs, 109
Council for Learning Assistance and Developmental Education Associations, 50
Council for the Advancement of Standards, 107
Council of Learning Assistance and Developmental Education Associations, 115
Credit courses: developmental, 114
Credit-based learning assistance, 3
Curricula: academic preparation courses, 28; remedial program courses, 33–34; of two- and four-year colleges, 59–61

## D

Dame schools, 25
Definition and terminology in field of learning assistance, 10–11
Degree completion, 62, 77
Delta Project, 62
Democracy, Jacksonian, 27–28
Demographics: background differences among students, 34–35; composition of students, 30; entering student body, 39; federally defined, 37; subpopulations, 9
Department of Education, 47, 60, 109, 116–117
Developmental courses, 16–17, 65, 67–70; curtailment of, 19–20; efficacy studies on, 68–69; elimination of credit, 114; outsourcing, 47–48
Developmental education, 44–45

Hawthorne, Nathaniel, 26
Heritage syndrome, 8–9
Hierarchy of approaches to learning
    assistance, 81–82, 84–85
High school articulation, 76–77
Higher education: failure to complete, 15;
    role of learning assistance in, 9
Higher Education Funding Council for
    England, 39
History of learning assistance: Phase One
    (1600s to1820s), 23–26; Phase Two
    (1830s to 1860s), 26–30; Phase Three
    (1870s to mid-1940s), 30–34;
    developmental course offerings, 16–17;
    Phase Four (mid-1940s to 1970s),
    34–42; founding of first colleges, 23;
    Phase Five (1970s to mid-1990s),
    42–51; Phase Six (mid-1990s to
    present), 51–53; lack of knowledge
    about, 7–9; review of, 11; summary of
    phases of, 24
Howard Community College, 47

**I**

Improved learning principles, 87–88
Institutional mission differentiation, 18–20
Institutional requirements for change,
    80–85
Instructional best practices, 97–99
Instructors. *See* faculty/staff
International Reading Association, 50
Iowa State College, 31

**J**

Jacksonian democracy, 27–28
Johnson, Lyndon, 36, 37
*Journal of College Reading and Learning,* 48
*Journal of Developmental and Remedial
    Education,* 50
*Journal of Developmental Education*, 49, 50
Junior colleges. *See* community colleges

**K**

Kaizan, 87
Kaplan, Inc., 47–48, 66, 78
Kellogg Foundation, 50

Kingsborough Community College, 70
Kirkwood Community College, 93–94

**L**

Labeling students: negative perceptions
    from, 12; problems of, 11–12
Land-grant institutions, 14, 18
Language. *See* terminology and definitions
    in field of learning assistance
Leaders of learning assistance programs,
    3–4; support systems for, 50–51
Learning assistance centers (LACs), 42–44,
    71; change recommendations for,
    111–112; operation of, 52–53
Learning communities, 69–70, 73–74, 112
Learning communities as, 74
Learning experience: supplemental, 71–73
Learning paradigms, 52
Learning professionals, 50–51
Learning Services (LS), 94
Lees-McRae College, 44

**M**

Manifestations of learning assistance, 1–4
Maryland Higher Education Commission,
    47, 78
Maxwell, Martha, 52
Medical model, 38
Metacognitive approaches, 89
Mid-American Association for Educational
    Opportunity Program Personnel, 49
Minnesota State Colleges and Universities,
    79
Mission differentiation, 18–20, 85
Models in learning assistance: educational
    theories and pedagogies, 88–91; medical
    model, 38; model of accountability in
    Britain, 37–38; public health model, 38;
    Wisconsin model, 29
MPR Associates, 41
Multiculturalism, 90–91, 97

**N**

National Association for Developmental
    Education (NADE), 49, 116; Self-
    Evaluation Guides, 107

National Association for
   Remedial/Developmental Studies, 49
National Association of Student Personnel
   Administrators, 118
National Center for Developmental
   Education (NCDE), 50
National Center for Education Statistics,
   21, 35, 55, 56, 58, 59, 60, 61, 62, 66,
   67, 68, 77
National centers for access, 117
National College Learning Center
   Association, 49
National Diffusion Network (NDN), 109,
   117
National Library of Education study, 18
National Louis University, 51, 107
National Reading Conference, 48–49
Necessary best practices, 102–104
Negative perceptions, 12
New York University, 28
No Child Left Behind, 78
Noel-Levitz Center, 44, 91, 103
Nomadic attendance, 77
Nontraditional students, 40

## O

Office of Educational Research and
   Improvement (OERI), 117
Offsetting enrollment, 30
Online courses for professionals, 115–116
Online tutoring, 78–80
Organizational best practices, 94–95
Origins of learning assistance, 23–25
Outcomes, 85; best practices affecting,
   98–99; likelihood of improved, 84
Out-of-class activities, 75
Outsourcing, 63; to commercial companies,
   78–80; of developmental courses,
   47–48; of learning assistance, 76–80; to
   other venues, 77–78
Oxford University, 25

## P

Part-time students, 35
Pedagogies, 88–91
Peer cognitive learning, 89

Peer-led team learning, 74–75
Perceptions, shifting, 9–18
Performance: gap between preparation and,
   32
Personnel. *See* faculty/staff
Phases of learning assistance programs. *See*
   history of learning assistance
Picked boys, 32
Pilot experiments, 47–48
Policies on learning assistance: change
   recommendations for policymakers,
   113–114, 116–117; institutional,
   102–104; state differences in, 19
Postsecondary education: history of
   learning assistance in, 7–9; mission
   differentiation issues, 20; segregation
   and stratification of, 16
Practitioners: support systems for, 50–51
Preparation: gap between performance and,
   32
Preparatory academies, 24, 28–29
Prerequisite acquisition approaches, 67–68
Princeton University, 33
Professional associations, 46–47, 102;
   change recommendations for, 114–115;
   rise of, 48–50
Professionals, learning assistance. *See*
   faculty/staff
Professionals in learning assistance: change
   recommendations for, 110–111
Program components, 95–97
Program Effectiveness Panel (PEP), 117
Program implementation research, 108
Provisional admissions, 16
Public health model, 38
Public policy issues, 15
Publications, professional, 111

## Q

Quality Assurance Agency, 46

## R

Recruitment of underprepared students, 24,
   30
Remedial programs, 65, 66–67; courses in
   curriculum, 33–34; curtailment of, 42;

description of, 45; history of, 27, 31–32, 66–67
Reporting systems, 56
Research: recommendations for future, 106–110
Resources: synergy of, 115
Retention, student, 102–103
Revenues: building institutional, 21
Review of Research in Development, 50
Rights of students, 13–16
Roles of learning assistance, 1–4, 7, 53; future approaches, 118

**S**

SAT scores, 21, 97
Secondary education: efficacy of, 9; poor/nonexistent, 27
Segregation of postsecondary education, 16
Selective admission policies, 15, 60
Services: direct provision of, 95; disproportionate impact of, 14; duplication of, 50; motivation of students to use, 97
Situated cognition, 89
SmartThinking, 78
South Carolina College, 30
Southwest Reading Conference, 48–49
Standards, 104; Council for the Advancement of Standards, 107; national, 104
Stanford University, 53
State mandates: elimination of developmental courses, 16–17
State policymakers: change recommendations for, 113–114
Stereotypes, 26
Stigma factors, 7, 12–13, 18, 34–35; for students using services, 54; terminology-related stigmas, 52
Stratification of postsecondary education, 16
Students: adult, 20; background differences among, 34–35; composition of populations of institutions, 30; diversity of, in learning assistance programs, 14–15, 51; emotions regarding learning

assistance of, 13; labeling, 11–12; motivation of, to use services, 97; nontraditional, 40; number of, using learning assistance, 55; older, 35; reasons for use of learning assistance by, 56; research on participation of, 108; retention of, 102–103; rights of, 13–16; subpopulations of, 9; test scores of underprepared, 39–40; theories that guide behavior of, 89
Supplemental learning experience, 71–73, 92
Support systems: for leaders/practitioners, 50–51
Swirling, 77
Sylvan Learning Systems, 47–48, 66, 78
Systems of learning assistance. *See* approaches to/systems of learning assistance

**T**

Talent development theory, 90
Target classes, 63, 73–75, 73–76
Task forces, 113
Tax issues: public taxes and learning assistance, 20–21; spending tax dollars on academic preparation, 18
Teaching and learning center operations, 52
Teaching paradigms, 52
Team learning: peer-led, 74–75
Technical colleges, 17
Terminology and definitions in field of learning assistance, 52, 118; descriptions of learning assistance, 10–12; establishing common vocabulary, 111; recommendations for changes in, 118
Test scores, 39–40
Texas State University at San Marcos, 51, 107
Theories, educational, 88–91; talent development theory, 90
Title III grants, 46
Title VI grants, 46
Towson University, 47
Traditional learning approaches, 37–38

Training and Certification of
    Developmental Educators, 50
Training for faculty/staff, 100
Transfer preparation programs, 17; barriers
    to success of, 18
TRIO programs, 36–37, 46, 49, 94
Tutoring programs, 72–73; efficacy study
    on, 72–73; history of, 23, 24; online,
    79; prevalence of, 25–26
Two-year public institutions, 67, 97

# U

Underprepared students: recruitment of,
    24, 30; test scores of, 39–40
United Kingdom (UK). *See* Britain/United
    Kingdom
United States: Commissioner for
    Education, 33; education movement in,
    28; history of colleges, 23; learning
    assistance programs compared to U.K.
    access programs, 46; Office of
    Education, 36–37; scope of learning
    assistance programs in, 56–61
Universal Instructional Design (UID),
    89–90, 98, 109
Universities and Colleges Admission
    Service, 46
University College Learning Center (Ball
    State University), 97
University of Alabama, 30
University of California, Berkeley, 74

University of Georgia, 30
University of Minnesota, 75–76, 79
University of Minnesota-Twin Cities, 51
University of Missouri, 16–17
University of Pennsylvania, 71–72
University of Texas, 91
University of Wisconsin, 28–29
Upper-level campus administrators: change
    recommendations for, 112–113
Upstream partnerships, 113
U.S. Department of Education, 47, 60,
    109, 116–117

# V

Valparaiso University, 30
Value-added perspective, 45, 111–112
Values, shifting, 9–18
Venues for learning assistance, 77–78

# W

War on Poverty, 37
Weingarten Learning Resource Center, 72
Western College Reading Association, 48
What Works Clearinghouse, 109
Williams College, 26
Wisconsin model of learning assistance, 29

# Y

Yale University, 25, 26, 33

# About the Author

**David R. Arendale** is an associate professor in the Department of Postsecondary Teaching and Learning in the College of Education and Human Development at the University of Minnesota–Twin Cities. He investigates access and learning assistance in postsecondary education, developing evidence-based strategies to increase academic success and persistence of underrepresented college students. At the University of Missouri–Kansas City, he served as national proj-ect director of supplemental instruction. In 1996 Arendale was elected president of the National Association for Developmental Education. The Council of Learning Assistance and Developmental Education Associations inducted Arendale as a founding fellow of the profession in 2000.

# About the ASHE Higher Education Report Series

Since 1983, the ASHE (formerly ASHE-ERIC) Higher Education Report Series has been providing researchers, scholars, and practitioners with timely and substantive information on the critical issues facing higher education. Each monograph presents a definitive analysis of a higher education problem or issue, based on a thorough synthesis of significant literature and institutional experiences. Topics range from planning to diversity and multiculturalism, to performance indicators, to curricular innovations. The mission of the Series is to link the best of higher education research and practice to inform decision making and policy. The reports connect conventional wisdom with research and are designed to help busy individuals keep up with the higher education literature. Authors are scholars and practitioners in the academic community. Each report includes an executive summary, review of the pertinent literature, descriptions of effective educational practices, and a summary of key issues to keep in mind to improve educational policies and practice.

The Series is one of the most peer reviewed in higher education. A National Advisory Board made up of ASHE members reviews proposals. A National Review Board of ASHE scholars and practitioners reviews completed manuscripts. Six monographs are published each year and they are approximately 120 pages in length. The reports are widely disseminated through Jossey-Bass and John Wiley & Sons, and they are available online to subscribing institutions through Wiley InterScience (http://www.interscience.wiley.com).

## Call for Proposals

The ASHE Higher Education Report Series is actively looking for proposals. We encourage you to contact one of the editors, Dr. Kelly Ward (kaward@wsu.edu) or Dr. Lisa Wolf-Wendel (lwolf@ku.edu), with your ideas.

# Recent Titles

ASHE HIGHER EDUCATION REPORT

# ORDER FORM SUBSCRIPTION AND SINGLE ISSUES

## DISCOUNTED BACK ISSUES:

Use this form to receive 20% off all back issues of *ASHE Higher Education Report*.
All single issues priced at **$23.20** (normally $29.00)

| TITLE | ISSUE NO. | ISBN |
|---|---|---|
| | | |
| | | |
| | | |

*Call 888-378-2537 or see mailing instructions below. When calling, mention the promotional code JBXND to receive your discount. For a complete list of issues, please visit www.josseybass.com/go/aehe*

## SUBSCRIPTIONS: (1 YEAR, 6 ISSUES)

☐ New Order    ☐ Renewal

| | | |
|---|---|---|
| U.S. | ☐ Individual: $174 | ☐ Institutional: $244 |
| Canada/Mexico | ☐ Individual: $174 | ☐ Institutional: $304 |
| All Others | ☐ Individual: $210 | ☐ Institutional: $355 |

*Call 888-378-2537 or see mailing and pricing instructions below.*
*Online subscriptions are available at www.interscience.wiley.com*

## ORDER TOTALS:

Issue / Subscription Amount: $ _____

Shipping Amount: $ _____
*(for single issues only – subscription prices include shipping)*

**Total Amount:** $ _____

| SHIPPING CHARGES: | | |
|---|---|---|
| | SURFACE | DOMESTIC CANADIAN |
| First Item | $5.00 | $6.00 |
| Each Add'l Item | $3.00 | $1.50 |

*(No sales tax for U.S. subscriptions. Canadian residents, add GST for subscription orders. Individual rate subscriptions must be paid by personal check or credit card. Individual rate subscriptions may not be resold as library copies.)*

## BILLING & SHIPPING INFORMATION:

☐ **PAYMENT ENCLOSED:** *(U.S. check or money order only. All payments must be in U.S. dollars.)*

☐ **CREDIT CARD:** ☐ VISA  ☐ MC  ☐ AMEX

Card number _____ Exp. Date _____

Card Holder Name _____ Card Issue # *(required)* _____

Signature _____ Day Phone _____

☐ **BILL ME:** *(U.S. institutional orders only. Purchase order required.)*

Purchase order # _____
          Federal Tax ID 13559302 • GST 89102-8052

Name _____

Address _____

Phone _____ E-mail _____

Copy or detach page and send to:  **John Wiley & Sons, PTSC, 5th Floor**
**989 Market Street, San Francisco, CA 94103-1741**

Order Form can also be faxed to:  **888-481-2665**

PROMO JBXND

## ASHE-ERIC HIGHER EDUCATION REPORT IS NOW AVAILABLE ONLINE AT WILEY INTERSCIENCE

## What is Wiley InterScience?

*Wiley InterScience* is the dynamic online content service from John Wiley & Sons delivering the full text of over 300 leading scientific, technical, medical, and professional journals, plus major reference works, the acclaimed Current Protocols laboratory manuals, and even the full text of select Wiley print books online.

## What are some special features of Wiley InterScience?

*Wiley Interscience Alerts* is a service that delivers table of contents via e-mail for any journal available on Wiley InterScience as soon as a new issue is published online.

*Early View* is Wiley's exclusive service presenting individual articles online as soon as they are ready, even before the release of the compiled print issue. These articles are complete, peer-reviewed, and citable.

*CrossRef* is the innovative multi-publisher reference linking system enabling readers to move seamlessly from a reference in a journal article to the cited publication, typically located on a different server and published by a different publisher.

## How can I access Wiley InterScience?

Visit http://www.interscience.wiley.com.

*Guest Users* can browse Wiley InterScience for unrestricted access to journal Tables of Contents and Article Abstracts, or use the powerful search engine. *Registered Users* are provided with a *Personal Home Page* to store and manage customized alerts, searches, and links to favorite journals and articles. Additionally, Registered Users can view free Online Sample Issues and preview selected material from major reference works. *Licensed Customers* are entitled to access full-text journal articles in PDF, with select journals also offering full-text HTML.

## How do I become an Authorized User?

*Authorized Users* are individuals authorized by a paying Customer to have access to the journals in Wiley InterScience. For example, a University that subscribes to Wiley journals is considered to be the Customer.

Faculty, staff and students authorized by the University to have access to those journals in Wiley InterScience are Authorized Users. Users should contact their Library for information on which Wiley journals they have access to in Wiley InterScience.

## ASK YOUR INSTITUTION ABOUT WILEY INTERSCIENCE TODAY!

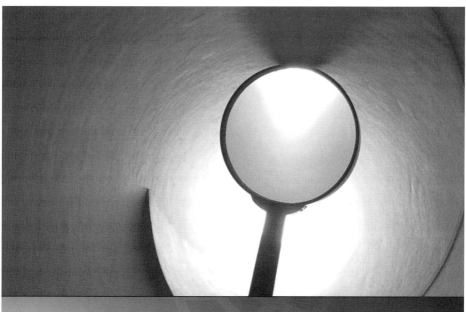

# YOUR free ISSUE OF
## NATIONAL CIVIC REVIEW
is now available online. Go to
www.interscience.wiley.com/journal/NCR

## In this Issue:

- Public Employees as Partners in Performance: Lessons From the Field *by Brooke A. Myhre*
- Starting Performance Measurement From Outside Government in Worcester *by Roberta Schaefer*
- Current Approaches to Citizen Involvement in Performance Measurement and Questions They Raise *by Anne Spray Kinney*
- Bridging the Divide Between Community Indicators and Government Performance Measurement *by Ted Greenwood*

**WILEY**
*Publishers Since 1807*